GIVE ME A FAITH LIKE THAT!

Walking In The Footsteps of Old Testament Saints

Sheila Alewine
www.aroundthecornerministries.org

Around The Corner Ministries exists to take the gospel to every neighborhood in America. Our mission is to equip followers of Jesus to engage their neighborhoods and communities with the gospel of Jesus Christ.

© 2022 by Sheila Alewine

ISBN: 978-1-7330478-8-3

Except where indicated, Scripture quotations taken from the New American Standard Bible® (NASB), Copyright © 1960, 1962, 1963, 1968, 1971, 1972, 1973, 1975, 1977, 1995, 2020 by The Lockman Foundation. Used by permission. www.Lockman.org.

A Word To The Reader

Now these things happened to them as an example,
and they were written for our instruction,
upon whom the ends of the ages have come.
–1 Corinthians 10:11

One of the things I look forward to the most in heaven, after seeing Jesus face to face and thanking Him for what He did for all of us, is meeting the people we read about in scripture. I am blessed to have grown up hearing and reading so many of the wonderful Bible stories that make up the heritage of faith passed down to us. I've often said I hope there is a large library of actual video footage of the events we read about for us to enjoy. Some may think we won't care about what happened on earth anymore, but these stories are so much a part of us and how we understand the character and nature of God, I'd like to think we'll get to explore them in a more personal way.

Do you have a favorite Bible character who you're looking forward to meeting? Whether it's the more famous saints like Daniel or David or the apostle Paul, or you're curious to talk with those whose names are only mentioned in passing, it's exciting to know we'll have eternity to finally have some questions answered. More importantly, we'll be able to thank these individuals for the treasures of wisdom and hope their lives provide for us, as we walk in faith just as they did.

God is so gracious to preserve His Word, not only the doctrines and theology that guide our faith, but the unique historical records of ordinary men and women through whom He has written the narrative of Jesus' story. Like Moses, each one had their own "burning bush" experience where they had to decide if they would walk by faith in the Creator and His infallible promises, or trust in their own knowledge, depending on sight and emotion.

How will you respond when God calls to you in your desperate circumstances? What will sustain you when all that you feel and know lets you down? You must respond in faith, believing what God says. You must build your life on the unshakeable foundation you can only see with the firm conviction that He is who He says He is, and He will do exactly what He says He will do.

My prayer is that over the next forty days, your faith will be encouraged, renewed, sustained, and inspired. We have a role to play in God's story, too. Ours may not be written down in scripture, but it is significant and important as we pass on our faith in the gospel of Jesus Christ to those around us. Let us be faithful to learn our lessons well from those who lived before us, until we all stand around God's throne, a thousand generations together worshipping the One in whom our faith rests.

Thank you for taking this journey with me. I am praying for you!

Sheila Alewine

4

The road is rugged, and the sun is hot.
How can we be but weary?

Here is grace for the weariness –
grace which lifts us up and invigorates us;
grace which keeps us from fainting by the way;
grace which supplies us with manna from heaven,
and with water from the smitten rock.

We receive of this grace, and are revived.
Our weariness of heart and limb departs.
We need no other refreshment.
This is enough.

Whatever the way be
– rough, gloomy, unpleasant –
we press forward,
knowing that the same grace
that has already carried thousands through
will do the same for us.

Horatius Bonar

DAY 1: GIVE ME A FAITH LIKE ADAM

Now the man called his wife's name Eve,
because she was the mother of all the living.
–Genesis 3:20

Faith Examined

Adam knew God personally in ways that you and I have not yet experienced. For a time, he was literally the only man on earth, living in holy fellowship with the One who had formed him from the dust, leaned close, and breathed into him the breath of life.

God saw that Adam needed a companion, another living soul like himself, unlike the animals that populated the garden. Adam underwent the very first surgery – God gave him divine anesthesia and took out a rib, shaped it into a woman, and presented her to Adam as his perfect counterpart. They spent their days cultivating the garden, catching up with God as they walked with Him in the cool of the day.

On the surface, Adam seems an unlikely candidate for a book about faith. After all, he and Eve are to blame for the beginning of our troubles with sin. While we're all responsible for our own personal sin, it was Eve who took the first step of disobedience, then turned to her husband and invited him to participate in mankind's first-ever rebellion against the Creator. Scripture tells us that Eve was deceived. Adam, on the other hand, took the offered fruit with full knowledge that he was sinning against God (1 Timothy 2:14).

We can speculate on his reasons. He loved his wife more than God? He was too weak to stand up against her willful decision? Ultimately, he chose his own wisdom over God's command – for just a moment, his faith failed him. Not only did he pay the price, the cost of his failure (death as the wages of sin) would be handed down to every human born from that moment on.

Though he stumbled in his faith walk, Adam did not turn his back on God entirely. Immediately after hearing the punishment for his sin, we find a faith-filled verse of hope in Genesis 3:20. *Adam called his wife's name Eve, because she was the mother of all the living.*

They had just received a sentence of physical death, yet in Eve's name, we see the hope of future life. Somehow, some day, God would bring *life* out of death. Those condemned to die because of sin would be given the chance to be redeemed through the promised Savior, Jesus, who would bruise the head of the serpent, the devil who had tempted Eve (Genesis 3:15).

Faith Enacted

Adam and Eve's faith in God had every opportunity to derail. After leaving the garden, they produced two sons, Cain and Abel. They didn't get a "happily ever after" story. The effects of the sin nature passed down to children now made in their image (Genesis 5:3) were brutal; Cain was jealous and murdered his brother. Yet Adam persevered in his faith, and we see that in his grandson's lifetime, men began to call upon the name of the Lord (Genesis 4:26). Adam passed on the lessons learned in the garden. He owned up to his failure of faith, and refused to abandon the object of his faith, the God who created him and loved him.

Adam's faith shows us two things. First, no matter how close or intimate we are with God, we still possess the free will and inclination to forsake what we know to be true and fail in our faith. Second, no matter how far we fall, God offers hope and reconciliation. He provided a way for our faith to be restored. He picks us up, sets our feet on the firm foundation of His grace and mercy, and calls us to keep walking in faith.

Have you failed in your faith? Welcome to the human race. Like Adam, we all must come out from behind the trees where we are hiding and admit our failures to the One who already knows them. Jesus came to restore our faith and bring us back to the Garden where we can walk with God once again.

Romans 5:19,21 – *For as through the one man's disobedience the many were made sinners, even so through the obedience of the One the many will be made righteous...so that, as sin reigned in death, even so grace would reign through righteousness to eternal life through Jesus Christ our Lord.*

Faith Expressed

Dear Father, Thank You for giving us hope even at the moment of Adam's failure. Your promise of a coming rescue gave Adam the strength to tell his children and grandchildren that faith in You was the only right response. He taught them to bring offerings, and to call on Your name. He trusted You to bring something good from what looked hopeless in his eyes. Help us when we stumble in our faith. Give us the courage to admit our failures, abandon our sin, and put our faith back where it belongs – in You. In Jesus' Name, Amen.

Day 2: Give Me A Faith Like Enoch

By faith Enoch was taken up so that he would not see death;
AND HE WAS NOT FOUND BECAUSE GOD TOOK HIM UP;
for before he was taken up, he was attested to have been pleasing to God.
–Hebrews 11:5

Faith Examined

There are only two people mentioned by name in the Bible who by-passed death and were transferred directly from this physical realm to the spiritual realm, into the presence of God: Enoch and Elijah. We'll leave Elijah's story for another day. Today, we are examining the kind of faith Enoch was said to have – a faith that God found both distinctive and pleasing.

Enoch is the sixth generation from Adam, and incidentally, Adam was still living and in the prime of his life at around age 622 when Enoch was born (Adam lived 930 years). The early patriarchs who lived before the flood of Noah's day were blessed with extremely long lives, averaging 900+ years. Enoch was the exception. At age 365, *he was not, for God took him* (Genesis 5:24). Enoch was the great-grandfather of Noah, and Enoch's firstborn son, Methuselah, holds the record for the longest life, living to the age of 969. Interestingly, the flood began the same year Methuselah died. This tells us a little about the culture in which Enoch lived, for by the time Noah was commanded to build the ark, the earth's inhabitants were so wicked God decided to destroy them all, save Noah and his family.

Enoch had a reputation that outlived him. Scripture says *Enoch walked with God*, and that God took him up because *he was attested to have been pleasing to God.* What, specifically, pleased God? Hebrews 11:6 tells us in context of Enoch's testimony. *And without faith it is impossible to please Him, for he who comes to God must believe that He is and that He is a rewarder of those who seek Him.*

Enoch's faith in God had two defining characteristics that pleased God; these two beliefs were central to his walk with God. We, too, can have faith like Enoch, by believing in the same way.

Belief #1 – We must believe that God is.

Atheism is the absence of faith that God exists. It is a denial of what God has revealed about Himself, His character, His attributes, and His very essence. Romans 1:20 tells us that the creation itself gives enough evidence to garner faith in God. Simply by observing the natural order of the world we live in, we see evidence of God's invisible attributes, His divine nature, and His eternal power. Enoch believed that God exists, and that He is who He says He is.

God-pleasing faith begins with believing God exists, and that He is who He claims to be. As Bible scholar Matthew Henry observed, *the practical belief of the existence of God, as revealed in the word, would be a powerful awe-band upon our souls, a bridle of restraint to keep us from sin, and a spur of constraint to put us upon all manner of gospel obedience* (Matthew Henry Commentary).

Belief #2 – We must believe that God rewards those who seek Him.

Faith that pleases God goes farther than intellectual acknowledgment of His existence. Many religious and non-religious people acknowledge the fact there must be a God, but those who place their faith *in God* are the ones who receive the reward of knowing Him personally. We must respond to God in faith by seeking Him in the one way He has prescribed: through His Son, Jesus Christ (John 14:6).

I believe this is the key belief that defined Enoch as a man who "walked with God." He moved beyond a superficial, intellectual assent to God's existence and pursued knowing Him personally and intimately. He *sought after* God. He desired God. He made it his life's ambition to do what pleased God.

Faith Enacted

Enoch's story engages my imagination because I love the possibility of escaping death. Enoch was "taken up," or "translated." He simply ceased to exist in this world. I've heard it expressed that one day, Enoch went out for a walk with God, and they had such a wonderful time together that God said, "Enoch, you're closer to My house than yours; why don't you just come on home with Me?" One can only wonder what his family and friends concluded!

What if we lived every day with unshakeable, God-pleasing faith in His eternal existence? What if we walked with Him minute by minute, knowing without a doubt that He is who He claims to be, and that every word He has spoken is true? What if we spent our time seeking to know Him more and more, fully convinced that hidden in Him are all the treasures of wisdom and knowledge? We will find that He alone is the true reward – the only One who can satisfy our soul's desires.

Do you have faith like Enoch?

1 Thessalonians 4:1 – *Finally then, brothers and sisters, we request and urge you in the Lord Jesus, that as you received instruction from us as to how you ought to walk and please God (just as you actually do walk), that you excel even more.*

Faith Expressed

Dear Father, We want to be people who please You! Give us faith like Enoch to believe You are who You say You are, and faith that diligently seeks after You. May we walk with You in faith and be counted worthy to be taken up one day, just like Enoch. In Jesus' Name, Amen.

DAY 3: GIVE ME A FAITH LIKE NOAH

> But Noah found favor in the eyes of the Lord.
> –Genesis 6:8

Faith Examined

One Bible scholar estimates there are more than 270 "flood legends" in various cultures of the world. While the details have changed as stories were passed down from generation to generation, all of these stories share common elements. We are blessed to have the inerrant Word of God to tell us the true, original version. In Genesis 6-9, we have the personal account inspired by the Holy Spirit – a front row seat to the actual events surrounding Noah and the worldwide flood.

Noah's world was much like ours today. Violence, lawlessness, moral depravity, and evil thoughts were the norm. God looked down at the sinful corruption of the beautiful creation and was sorry He had made man. He was grieved in His heart. The only solution He saw was to destroy every living thing He had made and begin again.

God chose to use a simple, ordinary man of faith to preserve the human race and give the world the opportunity for a "do-over." Noah's faith was exemplary for three reasons.

#1 – Noah refused to compromise in godly character.

Surrounded by unrelenting, overwhelming unrighteousness, *Noah found favor in the eyes of the Lord.* The Bible describes his character as a righteous man, blameless in his time; he was a man who walked with God (Genesis 6:9).

Righteous is also translated as "just," meaning lawful, righteous in conduct and character, correct. The law of Moses had not yet been written. All Noah had was the spiritual truth that had been handed down to him by his ancestors, but what a heritage that was! He was nine generations from Adam, but Adam had died just 126 years earlier. Adam's son, Seth, was *still alive when Noah was born.* No doubt Noah sat at the feet of his grandparents who heard of the events in the Garden of Eden first-hand from Adam and Eve.

Noah was blameless, also translated as "perfect." We know Noah was not sinless (Romans 3:23), but God had his *whole heart.* He was a man of integrity, completely given to serving God. He *walked with God*, indicating a personal, daily, intimate relationship with His Creator. His godly character was a product of his unwavering faith and trust in God.

#2 – Noah refused to compromise God's good commands.

Most of us can't fully comprehend the magnitude of the task God gave to Noah. Up to this point, no rain had fallen. There were no oceans nearby big enough to float the massive vessel God was describing. God gave Noah intricate, specific details for building the ark – the size, the materials, the shape, and the purpose. Noah had to plan for hundreds of animals – food, waste removal, and safety, as well as provide for the needs of his family. There's no record that God told Noah how long he would be on the ark. Noah had to listen carefully to God's detailed commands and follow them exactly if they were to survive.

God chose Noah because he knew his faith would not allow him to compromise on even one of God's good commands. *Noah did according to all that the Lord had commanded him* (Genesis 7:5).

#3 – Noah refused to compromise God's glorious cause.

Noah and his family spent just over a year in the ark. When God finally gave the "all clear" to step out into a world washed clean, Noah's immediate response and first action was to build an altar and offer sacrifices to worship God in gratitude for His salvation. A faithless man would have seen this as an opportunity to build his own kingdom. Not so for Noah. He wanted nothing more than to continue his life of walking with, and worshipping God.

God gave Noah the same commands He had given to Adam and Eve a thousand years earlier. He and his sons were to be fruitful, multiply and populate the earth, and subdue the animal kingdom. God made a new covenant with Noah to never again destroy all flesh or bring another worldwide flood. He set His bow in the sky as a sign of His promise.

Faith Enacted

Do you have faith like Noah? Are you uncompromising in godly character? Are you committed to fully obeying God? Is your life focused on worshipping God alone, even in the midst of a corrupt generation?

Noah's faith shows us that we can live pleasing to God no matter what the circumstances are around us. Uncompromising faith finds favor with God. Give me a faith like that.

Hebrews 11:7 – *By faith Noah, being warned by God about things not yet seen, in reverence prepared an ark for the salvation of his household, by which he condemned the world, and became an heir of the righteousness which is according to faith.*

Faith Expressed

Dear Father, Thank You for Noah's example. He gives us hope that we can be faithful even as our world is fast becoming "just as it was in the days of Noah," as Your word tells us will happen. Give us uncompromising faith in our character, our obedience, and our worship of You. In Jesus' Name, Amen.

Day 4: Give Me A Faith Like Abraham

All these died in faith, without receiving the promises,
but having seen them and having welcomed them from a distance,
and having confessed that they were strangers and exiles on the earth.
–Hebrews 11:13

Faith Examined

Abraham is the most well-known patriarch of the Hebrew faith, and by spiritual birth, the father of all who become his spiritual children through Christ (Romans 4:13-17). He and his wife, Sarah, are given premium space in the Hebrews 11 hall of fame; their story covers twelve verses, more than any other Old Testament saint. Abraham's faith is the stuff of legends.

Abraham's story begins in Genesis 12 when the Lord calls him as a 75-year-old man to leave his homeland of Ur. He begins a journey of trusting God to fulfill the promises He made in supernatural ways, until his death at the ripe old age of 175. He was an ordinary man God used to build the nation through whom our Savior came. Like a highlight reel, Hebrews 11 shines the spotlight on three aspects of Abraham's faith that allowed God to use him to impact the world.

#1 – Abraham's faith in God did not require all the details.

Hebrews 11:8 – *By faith Abraham, when he was called, obeyed by going out to a place which he was to receive for an inheritance; and he went out, not knowing where he was going.*

How would you respond if God asked you to pack up your home, your spouse, and your relatives, and move with no idea where you are going or what to expect when you get there? The lack of a clear, defined plan and expected outcome would cause us to think twice before obeying. While Abraham might have had questions in his heart and mind, he didn't hesitate to obey. God's command was clear; that was the only detail he needed.

#2 – Abraham's faith was focused on his eternal future, not his momentary present.

Hebrews 11:9-10 – *By faith he lived as an alien in the land of promise, as in a foreign land, dwelling in tents with Isaac and Jacob, fellow heirs of the same promise; for he was looking for the city which has foundations, whose architect and builder is God.*

For one hundred years, Abraham lived as a nomad in tents, traveling from place to place as his feet walked the land that God would one day give his descendants as an inheritance. God had promised to make him a great nation, to bless all the families of the earth through him. He never saw those promises fulfilled, but his faith remained firm. He knew God worked in the spiritual realm, and the physical realm was simply the scaffolding. The circumstances of his physical life never measured up to God's promises. Instead of a nation, Abraham had two sons, one of which he had to send away. He lived his whole life as an alien and a stranger in a land that didn't belong to him. If he had measured God's faithfulness by what he could see with his physical eyes, he would have missed the promises entirely. He chose to put his faith in the spiritual, what he could not see, but that was as real to him as his own flesh and blood.

#3 – Abraham's faith revealed a right view of God's power and authority.

Hebrews 11:17-19 – *By faith Abraham, when he was tested, offered up Isaac, and he who had received the promises was offering up his only begotten son; it was he to whom it was said, "In Isaac your descendants shall be called." He considered that God is able to raise people even from the dead, from which he also received him back as a type.*

Abraham's most famous "faith test" was the day God sent him up to the mountain to sacrifice the promised heir, Isaac. All of God's promises were wrapped up in Isaac, the miracle child born to him and Sarah in their old age. By this time, perhaps forty years after God had called him out of Ur, Abraham knew God's voice very well. There was no mistaking what God was asking him to do. By faith, Abraham obeyed. He bound his son to the altar and drew back his hand to plunge the knife in his heart, fully surrendered to God's authority and fully believing that God had the power to raise him from the dead. His faith never wavered because He had a right understanding of the nature and character of God.

Faith Enacted

Can we have faith like Abraham? That's asking a lot! Would we be willing to leave everything we know and follow God without all the necessary details that give us some assurance and expectations? Are we willing to let go of all the clutter and possessions that have our heart and live as a stranger and an alien, servants of a spiritual kingdom we cannot see? Is our faith grounded in a proper view of God's power and authority, or do we hesitate to release all our hopes and dreams for the people dearest to us to His greater plans?

Abraham's commitment and obedience inspires us to look beyond our physical circumstances and trust God, even when it makes no sense. Give me a faith like Abraham.

Hebrews 11:16 – *But as it is, they desire a better country, that is, a heavenly one. Therefore God is not ashamed to be called their God; for He has prepared a city for them.*

Faith Expressed

Dear Father, Thank You for the example of Abraham's faith. Our heart's desire is to have that same kind of trust in You, fully surrendering control over unknown details to the God who always keeps His promises. Give us the courage to trust You more than our fears, our hesitations, or our human logic. In Jesus' Name, Amen.

DAY 5: GIVE ME A FAITH LIKE SARAH

> By faith even Sarah herself received ability to conceive,
> even beyond the proper time of life,
> since she considered Him faithful who had promised.
> –Hebrews 11:11

Faith Examined

What would you do if your spouse asked you to lie for them, not just once, but on two separate occasions? Would it make a difference if they said the lie was for your benefit – to protect you? This is just one of the unusual and challenging circumstances Sarah encountered as a result of her marriage to Abraham.

It's difficult to appreciate the faith Sarah had if we only look at her from our twenty-first century perspective. Her story is deeply enmeshed in Abraham's. In her culture, a woman's faith was exemplified by a gentle and quiet spirit. Let's put ourselves in her shoes.

Sarai is sixty-five when Abram tells her that God has instructed them to leave their home, family, and all that is familiar, and set off on a trip with no destination. God has made Abraham a promise; He will make from him a great nation and bless all the families of the earth through him, even though he is already seventy-five himself. At this point, Sarai's name was not mentioned. As she is barren, she likely wonders what this prophecy means to her, but in obedience, she packs up their belongings and they set out towards Canaan.

Shortly afterwards, they find themselves in Egypt, hoping to avoid a famine. Abram knows the reputation of kings to take for themselves any beautiful woman they desired; he is afraid they will kill him for his wife, so he asks Sarai to lie and pretend to be his sister. Sarai agrees. Pharoah takes her into his house and treats Abram well, but God strikes his household with a plague to prevent any harm coming to Sarai. We find out later (when he does this again) Abram justifies his lie by the fact she is indeed his half-sister.

Ten years pass, and God renews His promise to give Abram a son but still doesn't mention Sarai. It was common practice in this culture for men to have children by multiple wives, so she suggests this might be God's plan, and Abram should try to have a child with her Egyptian maidservant. Abram agrees, and Hagar becomes pregnant. You can imagine how Sarai felt, especially when Hagar began to treat her with disrespect and contempt. She reacts out of hurt and regret, and banishes her from the camp, but the maid later returns in obedience to God and submits to Sarai's authority. The child, Ishmael, is born when Abram is eighty-six.

For thirteen years, Sarai lives in this complicated relationship, watching Abram grow to love Ishmael and believing she will never have a child. One day, God speaks to Abram, and initiates the covenant of circumcision. It's at this time He makes it clear that Sarai will be the mother of the promised child and changes both of their names to Abraham (father of a multitude) and Sarah (princess of multitudes). He then appears to both Abraham and Sarah, along with two angels, and affirms the promise that Sarah will have a child within the year. Knowing they are past the age of childbearing, Abraham and Sarah both laugh inwardly at this news. God challenges their disbelief, reminding them, *Is anything too difficult for the Lord?* (Genesis 18:14)

Sarah does indeed get pregnant and give birth to Isaac, whose name means "laughter." At his birth, Sarah declares, *God has made laughter for me; everyone who hears will laugh with me* (Genesis 21:6).

Though Isaac would appear to be her happy ending, the rest of Sarah's life was not without challenge. She gets angry with Ishmael for mocking Isaac and makes Abraham send him and his mother away. Also, when Isaac is a young man, she experiences a mother's worst nightmare as his father takes him up on a mountain to sacrifice him! Yet, in the end, she is listed in the Hebrews 11 hall of fame, as a woman of faith in the God who keeps His promises.

Faith Enacted

Sarah lived in a time when women had little choice but to obey their husbands and follow their wishes, even when they might disagree. This was Sarah's claim to faith – she had faith that God was faithful. While her decision to "help" God fulfill His promises brought her and Abraham an extra dose of heartache, ultimately, she was acting from a belief that if God had said it, it must be true.

Faith in God doesn't always look "spectacular" or do amazing things that bring attention to us. Sometimes faith is simply walking in quiet obedience along the path God puts us on, trusting Him to work out His sovereign plans. It's a submissive, humble attitude that trusts God to protect us even when those in authority over us might make a mistake or foolish decision. Sarah walked by faith in the circumstances and culture in which God had placed her. It's clear she was a woman who loved deeply, yet, like all of us, had moments of frustration, and emotional highs and lows. In the end, scripture testifies that she was faithful to believe God would do what He said He would do. Her real beauty was inward, the hidden person of a faithful heart.

1 Peter 3:3-6 – *Your adornment must not be merely external – braiding the hair and wearing gold jewelry, or putting on dresses; but let it be the hidden person of the heart, with the imperishable quality of a gentle and quiet spirit, which is precious in the sight of God. For in this way in former times the holy women also, who hoped in God, used to adorn themselves, being submissive to their own husbands; just as Sarah obeyed Abraham, calling him lord, and you have become her children if you do what is right without being frightened by any fear.*

Faith Expressed

Dear Father, Thank You for Sarah's example of a quiet and humble faith that submits to Your plans. May we find our hope in You, not our circumstances, and live in a way that reveals our faith in the God who is faithful to us. In Jesus' Name, Amen.

DAY 6: GIVE ME A FAITH LIKE ISAAC

> I appeal to you therefore, brethren, by the mercies of God,
> to present your bodies as a living sacrifice,
> holy and acceptable to God—
> this is a reasonable act of worship for you.
> –Romans 12:1 (*Mounce*)

Faith Examined

I wonder if Isaac ever felt pressure to "live up to" his father's faith. Of course, during his life he had no idea how famous Abraham would become as the esteemed patriarch of a nation. He couldn't see that his father's name would become synonymous with faith, or that his descendants would forever be God's chosen people.

To Isaac, he was just "Abba," his daddy, an ordinary man that had an extraordinary relationship with Jehovah God. I imagine Isaac loved hearing his parents talk about the unusual circumstances surrounding his birth, but I also think he must have felt the weight of being the "promised" child, one through whom God would keep His promises to his father.

We don't know exactly how old Isaac was when his father suggested they hike up Mount Moriah to present a burnt offering to the Lord. He was old enough to carry the load of wood for the offering, and to accompany his father on the three-day journey into the wilderness (Genesis 22:4-6). Bible scholars estimate he was at least an older teenager and could possibly have been a young man in his twenties or early thirties.

Halfway up the mountain, Isaac suddenly realizes they have brought no animals with them. He expresses no surprise at his father's response when questioned about this important detail. Abraham assures him, "God will provide for Himself the lamb for the burnt offering, my son" and the two of them walk on together towards the place of sacrifice (Genesis 22:8).

I can only speculate on Isaac's thoughts as they prepared the altar and arranged the wood. How long would they wait for the promised sacrifice to appear? We're not given any insight to the conversation that surely occurred when it dawned on Isaac that his father intended to sacrifice *him*. He was certainly old enough to protest – to resist – to refuse. He surely could have overpowered his father who by this time was well past one hundred years in age. The only detail we're given – what God wants us to see in Isaac's faith – is that he willingly allowed his hands to be bound and his body laid on the altar of sacrifice.

Isaac's willingness to go along with what his father assured him was God's will revealed that he also possessed a strong faith in God. I'm sure he loved his father, but that kind of obedience – the commitment to *literally* lay one's life down in obedience and sacrifice – could only be directed toward God. Isaac had seen God be faithful to his parents many times over. He knew that his very existence was a testimony to God's ability to keep His promises. It's not unreasonable to conclude that he assured his father with unshakeable confidence that God would indeed raise him from the dead, giving Abraham the courage to draw back the knife, fully prepared to plunge it into his son's heart.

Faith Enacted

Isaac's encounter on the mountain is a living example of the *reasonable act of worship* God expects of us – people who have also experienced the mercy of God through a substitute sacrifice.

Genesis 22:13 – *Then Abraham raised his eyes and looked, and behold, behind him a ram caught in the thicket by his horns; and Abraham went and took the ram and offered him up for a burnt offering in the place of his son.*

Paul often referred to Abraham's faith as proof that our salvation is purchased not by works, but by grace alone, through faith alone. He understood that Abraham's willingness to sacrifice his son was a picture of what God would do two thousand years later on Mount Calvary, when He offered His own beloved Son, Jesus *in our place*. Isaac's obedience in climbing on that altar as a living sacrifice is a visual for us – the reasonable response from a person who knows they owe their existence to the God who showed them mercy and indeed, brought the dead to life.

What is reasonable? The Greek word is *logikos*, meaning logical, rational, agreeable to reason. It is a mindful, intelligent decision of our will, just as Isaac agreeably and willingly put himself on the altar in response to God's command.

That's the kind of faith we want – faith that is willing to lay down our lives, no matter the cost, because *it's the only logical response* to what Jesus did for us. Give me a faith like that.

Romans 6:13 – *And do not go on presenting the members of your body to sin as instruments of unrighteousness; but present yourselves to God as those alive from the dead, and your members as instruments of righteousness to God.*

Faith Expressed

Dear Father, The world views faith as illogical, a crutch for the weak, but those of us who follow Jesus understand that faith is simply the only rational response to the truth of the gospel. Jesus laid down on the altar for us, and unlike Isaac, You didn't rescue Him from death. Jesus took the sharp blade of the cross all the way to the grave to put an end to sin and death for us. Give us faith like Isaac to live as resurrected people. We offer ourselves up to you in daily sacrifice, surrendered fully to Your perfect will. In Jesus' Name, Amen.

Day 7: Give Me A Faith Like Jacob

By faith Jacob, as he was dying, blessed each of the sons of Joseph,
and worshiped, leaning on the top of his staff.
–Hebrews 11:21

Faith Examined

Jacob's story makes up a large portion of the book of Genesis, starting with his birth in chapter 25 and ending with his death in chapter 49. God proclaimed his destiny while he was still in the womb. He would be the second-born of twins but receive the blessings and birthright as though he were the eldest (Genesis 25:23). God chose Jacob over his older brother, Esau, and made of him a great nation through whom the Son of God came in human flesh.

Romans 9:10-13 – *And not only this, but there was Rebekah also, when she had conceived twins by one man, our father Isaac; for though the twins were not yet born and had not done anything good or bad, so that God's purpose according to His choice would stand, not because of works but because of Him who calls, it was said to her, "The older will serve the younger." Just as it is written, "Jacob I loved, but Esau I hated."* (See also Malachi 1:1-5).

We would think that if God chose Jacob before he was born, He saw something worthwhile in him. That in His omniscience, He knew Jacob would faithfully serve Him in perfect obedience and was therefore the right choice. But that's not anywhere near how Jacob's life turned out. His story is one of grace upon grace; it's the picture of God accomplishing in and through him His own sovereign purposes *despite* Jacob's human weaknesses and tendencies for failure.

Jacob came out of the womb fighting for his position as he grasped his brother's heel, earning his name, which means "heel holder, supplanter, layer of snares, or deceiver." Scripture says the children struggled together in Rebekah's womb, and the conflict and competition between these two continued into the generations that followed. (Edom, the nation that descended from Esau, became a thorn in Israel's flesh.)

In today's language, we could call Jacob a "mama's boy," going along with her scheme to deceive Isaac and steal the father's blessing for his firstborn son. He stayed in the tents learning to cook, using the opportunity of his brother's hunger to trade a bowl of stew for his birthright.

Jacob did not move in a straight line towards faith in God. He and his father-in-law traded schemes and deceptions, and after twenty years of serving Laban, having his wages changed ten times, and being deceived into marrying a woman he did not love, he finally took his two wives, two concubines, eleven children, and the flocks and herds he had amassed and returned home. Throughout all of it, as Jacob struggled to learn to trust God's plans and timing, *God was faithful to him*, and blessed him abundantly. Jacob's life encourages us because it shows us that our ability to remain faithful and obedient is less important than God's faithfulness. God's mercy and compassion is greater than our lack of faith. He truly is able to work all things together for good when we love Him and are called according to His purposes (Romans 8:28).

Jacob did a lot of things that we might think disqualified him from the Hebrews 11 hall of fame, but God says differently by pointing out something Jacob did at the very end of his life. Hebrews 11:21 takes us back to Jacob's blessing over Joseph's two sons, Manasseh and Ephraim.

Genesis 48:15-16 – *He blessed Joseph, and said, "The God before whom my fathers Abraham and Isaac walked, the God who has been my shepherd all my life to this day, the angel who has redeemed me from all evil, bless the lads; and may my name live on in them, and the names of my fathers Abraham and Isaac; and may they grow into a multitude in the midst of the earth."*

At the end of his life, Jacob recognized that any good, any blessing, any worthwhile things that had come into his life or from his life ultimately came from God. It was God, who had appeared to him in visions and dreams, and had wrestled with him in his darkest and most fearful moments and redeemed his life from the poor choices he had made. This same God had changed his name from Jacob (*supplanter, heel grabber, deceiver*) and called him Israel (*God prevails*).

Faith Enacted

Do you look back on your life and only see failure? This perspective may bring us to the end of our days as bitter, regretful, and guilt-ridden old people who waste the final moments God gives us to pass on a blessing to the next generation.

We need faith like Jacob, who saw beyond his human weaknesses and trusted that God had made something worthwhile out of all his struggles. When he said, "May my name live on in them," he wasn't speaking of his own fame. He was passing on the blessing that he had taken a lifetime to learn – *God prevails.*

Psalm 103:13-17 – *Just as a father has compassion on his children, so the Lord has compassion on those who fear Him. For He Himself knows our frame; He is mindful that we are but dust. As for man, his days are like grass; as a flower of the field, so he flourishes. When the wind has passed over it, it is no more, and its place acknowledges it no longer. But the lovingkindness of the Lord is from everlasting to everlasting on those who fear Him, and His righteousness to children's children.*

Faith Expressed

Dear Father, How grateful we are that You prevail. You are bigger than our mistakes. Your infinite grace and mercy are able to take our weaknesses and striving to live pleasing to You and make good out of them, despite our failures. May we keep our eyes on You and trust You to make the end of our story all about Your faithfulness. In Jesus' Name, Amen.

Day 8: Give Me A Faith Like Joseph

Joseph named the firstborn Manasseh, "For," he said,
"God has made me forget all my trouble and all my father's household."
He named the second Ephraim "For," he said,
"God has made me fruitful in the land of my affliction."
–Genesis 41:51-52

Faith Examined

How do you deal with your past? Do you hold tightly to things that have happened to you, allowing them to continually influence your outlook on life? We are all products of our past, both the good and the bad. People and events leave their mark on our minds and hearts, and every experience shapes our attitudes. How we deal with our past determines if we spend our days in joy and peace, or in bitterness, unforgiveness, regret, anger, or depression.

Joseph was a man who had experienced a lot of harsh things, even from childhood. As his father's favorite, he received special treatment that alienated him from his brothers. God clearly had His hand on Joseph from the beginning, giving him dreams and visions of the future. Unfortunately, at seventeen he lacked the maturity to keep this special knowledge to himself, and relating his dreams came across as boastful, creating even more division between him and his siblings.

Joseph had every opportunity to become a bitter old man. His brothers threw him in a pit, then decided to sell him as a slave. He was convicted and sent to prison because he refused to commit adultery with his employer's wife. He was forgotten by the people he helped, and he spent twenty-two years of his adult life estranged and separated from his family. Yet in all this, his faith in God's sovereignty continued to grow.

Life got better for Joseph when the opportunity came to interpret Pharoah's dream. He was elevated to the highest position in the land, second in command only to Pharoah himself. This success did not come because Joseph worked hard and earned it. Joseph's success was rooted in his unfailing faith in God. In every uncomfortable and painful situation, we are told that Joseph advanced because God's hand was upon him.

As often happens in every life story, circumstances occurred that brought Joseph face to face with his past. In need of food, his father, Jacob, sends his ten brothers to Egypt to purchase grain from Pharoah's storehouse. It is Joseph, the brother they sold into slavery, who determines their fate. As they bow before the tall, imposing Egyptian ruler, they have no idea he is the scrappy seventeen-year-old brother whose death they faked, bringing much grief to their father.

Joseph can't resist giving his brothers a bit of a hard time, although he leaves the room at times to weep. His heart is overcome with the emotions of being reunited with his family. When he finally reveals himself, his brothers are deeply concerned that he will take his revenge on them. And why not? He has the position and the power; their lives are in his hands. They don't know that God has healed Joseph's heart and he has let go of all the pain in his past, surrendering it to the sovereignty and wisdom of God. In the moments of reunion, Joseph fully recognizes that all his suffering had a greater purpose, and that while the journey was painful, God had protected and sustained him through it for something good.

Genesis 50:19-20 – *But Joseph said to them, "Do not be afraid, for am I in God's place? As for you, you meant evil against me, but God meant it for good in order to bring about this present result to preserve many people alive."*

Faith Enacted

Joseph made peace with his past long before the opportunity came to make peace with his brothers. With the birth of his two sons, he declared that God had made him forget the troubles and those who had hurt him and made him fruitful in the midst of his afflictions (Genesis 41:51-52). As he explained it to his brothers years later, he was not "in God's place." Their sin was against God, and he had no right to withhold forgiveness. He trusted more in the sovereignty of God than in any man's ability to determine his fate. This decision of his will – to leave the past in God's hands and trust God to judge those who had wronged him – allowed him to move forward in life and enjoy the blessings and rewards of his faith.

How about you? Are there things in your past that you just can't seem to let go? Are there people who have hurt you deeply you still can't forgive? ***Are you in God's place?***

Ask God for a faith like Joseph. Step out of the way and trust God's sovereignty and wisdom in all of life – the good and the bad, the painful and the pleasant, the success and the failure. Let God bring good out of what others meant for evil. We can't control what happens to us, but with faith in God's grace and the Holy Spirit's help, we can control what we do with it.

Romans 8:28 – *And we know that God causes all things to work together for good to those who love God, to those who are called according to His purpose.*

Faith Expressed

Dear Father, We live in a sinful, fallen world, and pain is an inevitable part of my life. I have hurt others, and others have hurt me in return. People make choices that result in broken relationships and regret. You are the only one who can take mistakes and messes and create something beautiful and good from them. Help me to see my life – the good and the bad – through the lens of Your sovereignty and wisdom, and to trust You enough to let go of anything that keeps me in Your place. You are God, and I am not, and I trust You more. In Jesus' Name, Amen.

DAY 9: GIVE ME A FAITH LIKE MOSES

Know therefore today, and take it to your heart,
that the Lord, He is God in heaven above
and on the earth below;
there is no other.
–Deuteronomy 4:39

Faith Examined

Moses is one of the most well-known and beloved saints in the Old Testament, perhaps because scripture gives so many details about him. All of us can see ourselves in him at different places of his life's journey. His very birth was an affront to the ruling class of Egyptians and according to Pharoah's decree, he would never have been allowed to live. His mother's plan to hide him, no doubt prompted by God's sovereign hand, resulted in his being brought up as the original "third culture kid" – someone who is raised in a different culture than their parents or their own nationality.

Moses was a Hebrew raised as an Egyptian prince. When he became aware of his heritage, he began to see his people's burdens. He took matters into his own hands and killed an Egyptian master while trying to defend a Hebrew slave. He then ran away to escape the murder charge. For the next forty years, Moses hid in the wilderness, tending sheep while God tended his heart to make him into the man he would use to free His people and bring them into the Promised Land.

Confronted by God at the burning bush, Moses' life took a new turn. He would spend the rest of his life watching God do supernatural, unbelievable things. He would also be asked to step out of his comfort zone and be the leader he did not want to be.

We identify with Moses because we can see the weak spots in his faith. He was an open book, never afraid to express his feelings to God, even at his lowest moments. God spoke to Moses face to face as a man speaks to his friend (Exodus 33:11). Yet in this intimate familiarity, Moses never lost his awe and respect for God; instead, he grew to understand God's holiness and justness in a very personal way.

Moses' faith wasn't perfect. He had the difficult job of leading an estimated two million souls through a wilderness for forty years, listening to their complaints and pleading with God for mercy when they foolishly disobeyed. We understand and empathize with Moses as he stands on the rock from which God will produce water a second time. God tells him to speak to the rock, but Moses is tired and frustrated, overwhelmed with his responsibilities, and frankly, fed up with being blamed for the hard journey. For just a moment, he gives way to his flesh and lifts his voice in anger toward the people: *Listen now, you rebels; shall **we** bring forth water for you out of this rock?* Not only that, but he strikes the rock twice (Numbers 20:8-11).

Immediately, two things happen. God does bring the water and the crowd's thirst is satisfied abundantly. And straightaway, He deals with Moses' outburst. The discipline for his disobedience is costly – he will not enter the Promised Land with the people but will die on the mountain as he looks over into what he would never possess.

"How unfair!" you might think. Doesn't Moses deserve a pass? It seems the price is too high. When Moses heard God's decision, I'm sure his heart sank, and he immediately regretted what he'd done. I'm positive he repented, because as he retells the story in Deuteronomy, he reminds the people that God is still just, still righteous, and still worthy to be worshipped, served, and obeyed. There is no other God, even when His justice feels unfair.

At the end of his life, God invited Moses up to the top of Mount Nebo and showed him all the land He would give to the children of Israel. By this time, Moses was 120 years old. What seemed like punishment perhaps turned out to be a blessing. God gave Moses rest from his work, passing his responsibilities as leader to Joshua, and took him home to the *real* Promised Land.

Faith Enacted

Moses reminds us of what it looks like to have real faith in God. It is continuing to trust Him when the outcome isn't what we wanted. It is accepting the consequences of our choices, having full confidence that God is fair and just and will bring good out of it. Faith is knowing God is worthy of our worship not because of what He does for us, but because of who He is.

Has your faith wavered because life hasn't turned out like you thought it would? Have you doubted that God is good, and fair, and right because His discipline seems harsh? Have faith like Moses. Trust God's heart. Trust His character. Seek His presence, not His permissiveness. The path may be long, but He will get you home.

> *For I proclaim the name of the Lord; ascribe greatness to our God!*
> *The Rock! His work is perfect, for all His ways are just;*
> *a God of faithfulness and without injustice,*
> *righteous and upright is He.*
> (The Song of Moses, Deuteronomy 32:3-4)

Faith Expressed

Dear Father, Moses was a man who walked with You; You called him Your friend. It encourages us to know that he was just like us, because he still had moments when his faith failed him. The best part of Moses' story is how much You truly loved him, even when You had to discipline him. He was Your faithful servant, trusting Your heart and Your righteous character. We love that You took time to meet with him on the mountain, and You took him home. You even buried His body. What a loving Father you are! Teach us to have faith like Moses. In Jesus' Name, Amen.

DAY 10: GIVE ME A FAITH LIKE JOSHUA

Thus the Lord used to speak to Moses face to face,
just as a man speaks to his friend.
When Moses returned to the camp,
his servant Joshua, the son of Nun, a young man,
would not depart from the tent.
–Exodus 33:11

Faith Examined

Who has shaped your faith? One of Christianity's defining characteristics is that of disciple-making, also referred to as "discipleship." When we come to faith in Christ, we begin a relationship with God that must be nurtured and grown. Jesus gave us the perfect example on how this should take place.

He spoke publicly to the multitudes, both believers and unbelievers.
He taught smaller groups of disciples who followed Him from place to place.
He invested in and developed a core group of twelve.
He intimately shared with three: Peter, James, and John.

Becoming a disciple requires mentorship. We need to spend time with more mature believers who can teach us both in God's word and personal example, help us develop our spiritual gifts, and encourage us in the sanctification process the Holy Spirit does in each of our hearts and minds as He transforms us into Christlikeness.

Joshua was a young man privileged to be mentored, discipled, and taught by one of the great saints of God – Moses. We don't know exactly when or how Joshua was selected to be the servant of Moses. He is first mentioned as assigned by Moses to lead the fight against the Amalekites in Exodus 17; the next time we see him, he accompanies Moses up to the mountain of God, disappearing with his mentor for forty days. Out of all the elders, including Aaron, only Joshua is allowed into this holy space to receive the Ten Commandments directly from God. I imagine he was also tasked with recording all the details God gave them for the sacrifices and Tabernacle construction.

Joshua will go down in history as a man who did great things for God. He and Caleb were the only two who believed God would give the people the land as He promised, and as a result, were the two men in their generation who saw the promise fulfilled. He took Moses' place to lead the children of Israel into Canaan. He brought the leadership necessary for each tribe to take possession and dispossess the land of their enemies. He had big shoes to fill when Moses died, and God affirmed him as the chosen leader before the congregation when He parted the Jordan River for the long-awaited entry into the Promised Land (Joshua 3:7).

What made Joshua's faith so strong, and positioned him to be used by God to accomplish His sovereign purposes?

Was it simply Moses' influence as an outstanding mentor, or was there something more?

I believe Joshua's secret to great faith was not only in having a wonderful mentor, but in a personal hunger for God. While Moses certainly shared the things he knew and experienced in his own walk with God, second-hand knowledge wasn't enough for Joshua. He pursued an intimate, personal, face-to-face relationship with God himself. We see this in Exodus 33:11. Joshua was present when God spoke face-to-face with Moses, as a man speaks to his friend, and he wasn't satisfied with just watching. He lingered in the tent, long after Moses had gone, spending time with God alone.

Faith Enacted

If we're not careful, discipleship can be reduced to passing on information and knowledge instead of introducing people to the Person of Jesus. Becoming a disciple is far more than memorizing the teachings of Christ. It is coming to know the Master Himself. It requires a willingness to stay behind when others leave, to linger in God's presence until the Holy Spirit brings the Word of God alive to us and we know we have been in His presence.

We no longer have to go out to the Tent of Meeting. The temple of God has come to us – *in us* – through the indwelling Holy Spirit of God. While we definitely need to be discipled and mentored by the mature believers, we are desperate to be taught by God through His Word, *personally.* Time with great saints is good; time with the Savior is essential.

Have you substituted time in God's Word for the words of others?
Are you following the followers of Jesus, or Jesus Himself?

Give me a faith like Joshua. No matter how wonderful or special my mentors are, they never take the place of Jesus and His Word. Let us linger in the tent until we meet with God face-to-face. Then, and only then, will we be ready for the work to which we are called.

Joshua 1:8-9 – *This book of the law shall not depart from your mouth, but you shall meditate on it day and night, so that you may be careful to do according to all that is written in it; for then you will make your way prosperous, and then you will have success. Have I not commanded you? Be strong and courageous! Do not tremble or be dismayed, for the Lord your God is with you wherever you go.*

Faith Expressed

Dear Father, I want faith in You like Joshua had, but I know that it comes with a cost. Help me to be patient and willing to spend time with You, to meditate on Your Word day and night, and be careful to obey it. May I not only seek knowledge about You that is passed on from others but may I know You personally as You speak to me through Your Word. In Jesus' Name, Amen.

DAY 11: GIVE ME A FAITH LIKE RAHAB

> By faith Rahab the harlot did not perish along with those who were
> disobedient, after she had welcomed the spies in peace.
> –Hebrews 11:31

Faith Examined

There's no way around the obvious truth about Rahab's lifestyle. We read her story in Joshua 2-6. The massive assembly of Israelites are poised to cross the Jordan River, finally ready to go in and possess the land as God promised them forty years earlier. The last of the rebellious generation has died out. Joshua takes up the mantle of Moses' command and sends two men in to spy out the first city they will battle, Jericho.

Rahab lives on the city wall, running a house of prostitution. Both the Old and New Testament describe her as a harlot, using the Hebrew word *zānâ* and the Greek word *pornē*, leaving no doubt as to her profession. The two spies take refuge in her house, the only place where their presence in the city would be less likely noticed. Rahab was an immoral woman, but she recognized immediately her only option. She knew without a doubt that the God of Israel would give the city into their hands, so she asked for mercy in exchange for hiding the men from the city officials.

The men agree; Rahab's act of faith exposed a heart change. Instead of stubbornly clinging to her past, she abandoned all loyalty to her old life and surrendered her future, placing her trust in the God these two men served. The men give her one simple instruction to secure her life and the lives of her family members. She must tie a cord of scarlet thread in the window and gather her loved ones under its protection. When the armies of Israel arrive, the scarlet cord will signify to the attackers that those inside are to be allowed to live; they will not suffer the coming judgment.

Immediately upon the departure of the spies, Rahab hangs the scarlet cord in her window. She knew it would take three days for them to return to their camp. She was fully aware that the massive amount of people had not crossed the Jordan. She surmised it would take a few days to make a battle plan. Yet, she did not delay in placing herself and her family under the protection of the scarlet cord. She did not know when her rescuers would arrive, but she wanted to be ready. She had committed her life into the hands of the God of Israel, and there was no turning back or hesitation.

Faith Enacted

That scarlet cord...what a beautiful picture of the sacrificial blood, not only of the Passover lambs that protected the last generation of Israelites from the angel of death sent to slay Egypt's firstborn, but a picture of the precious, saving blood of our Rescuer, Jesus. It's not random that the two spies chose a bright red cord to mark the house of a harlot who placed her faith in Jehovah. God doesn't do random. The scarlet cord is an intentional illustration that when we come to God, we come through the cross and the shed blood of our Savior. Only Jesus' blood is able to protect us from the wrath of God against sin.

When the armies of Israel brought Rahab and her family back to the camp, they were first brought only *outside* the camp (Joshua 6:23). As Gentiles, they were unclean; they would need a time of ceremonial cleansing before they were welcomed into the midst of God's people. *Outside the camp* is where the remains of the sin offering were taken, a picture of the place Jesus suffered *outside the gate* the day He died for the sins of the whole world (Hebrews 13:11-13). Two verses later we read that Rahab and her household *lived in the midst of Israel to this day* (Joshua 6:25). Her immediate, obedient, expectant faith in God brought her near as she embraced the commands and culture of her new family.

Rahab married a man named Salmon; they had a son named Boaz, who became the great-grandfather of King David. Trace that genealogy all the way to the New Testament, and we learn that Rahab is included in the ancestral line of our Savior, Jesus! A harlot in the line of Christ? Oh, yes, indeed. And aren't we grateful, because in our hearts, we were all adulterers, caught in our own sins, before the scarlet thread of redemption wove its way into our world, our lives, and rescued us from wrath.

Rahab's faith was a faith that acted immediately. She did not wait until she saw the armies assembled around the city and then scramble to hang the cord in time. When offered redemption and rescue, she made her decision without delay, anxious and relieved to be under the protection of the scarlet cord.

How's your faith? Have you heard the good news that God came to rescue you from your sin, but are delaying your decision because you don't see the need quite yet? Has your faith waned, and you've gone back to your old life, not seeing the need for fully committing just yet? Have faith like Rahab, who fully obeyed, immediately. Make a stop *outside the camp* to kneel at the cross, then come and gather with God's people. The only safe place, both from enemy attacks and God's judgment against sin, is in the shelter of the scarlet cord of the cross of Christ.

Hebrews 13:11-13 – For *the bodies of those animals whose blood is brought into the Holy Place by the high priest as an offering for sin are burned outside the camp. Therefore Jesus also suffered outside the gate, that He might sanctify the people through His own blood. So then, let us go out to Him outside the camp, bearing His reproach.*

Faith Expressed

Dear Father, How grateful we are for the blood of Christ. How thankful we are for its protection, both in this life, from the attacks of our enemy, and in the life to come as it offers us redemption and forgiveness from sin. May we draw near to Your cross, always mindful and grateful for the shed blood – our scarlet cord of safety that leads to eternal life. In Jesus' Name, Amen.

DAY 12: GIVE ME A FAITH LIKE CALEB

> But My servant Caleb, because he has had a different spirit
> and has followed Me fully, I will bring into the land which he entered,
> and his descendants shall take possession of it.
> –Numbers 14:24

Faith Examined

There are numerous attributes about Caleb's character that set him apart and earn our respect. Caleb's story spans two significant timeframes in Israel's history, a fact which is unique to him and just one other person, Joshua. Caleb was among the adults that experienced the dramatic, miraculous exodus from Egypt and the crossing of the Red Sea. He was an eyewitness to the miracles God did through Moses and Aaron, and he stood on the shore and watched as Pharoah and his army paid the ultimate price for hardening their hearts against God.

In Numbers 13-14, Caleb was one of ten men sent to spy out the land God was giving to them, but only he and Joshua had faith enough to believe God would do what He said. This unshakeable confidence in the character and promises of God enabled him to stand against the majority. As we know, the people rejected his advice, and so Caleb found himself in the second significant era of Israel's history. All his peers passed away in the wilderness and he and Joshua were the only adults over twenty years of age that entered the Promised Land.

Forty-five years later, Caleb's story comes centerstage again in Joshua 14. The Israelites have entered the land, and Joshua has begun assigning each tribe's allotment. It's worth noting that even when the land begins to be divided among Jacob's twelve sons, there are still cities and kings and cultures yet to conquer. God is giving them the title deed to what He promised, but the people have the responsibility to do the hard work and take hold of it.

Caleb has been waiting a long time for this day. At eighty-five, one would think he would surrender his portion to his children and simply live out his days in peace. Instead, he is excited by the challenge ahead and requests one of the more difficult conquests. The defining characteristic of his faith is still as strong as ever.

Joshua 14:7-9 – *I was forty years old when Moses the servant of the Lord sent me from Kadesh-barnea to spy out the land, and I brought word back to him as it was in my heart. Nevertheless my brethren who went up with me made the heart of the people melt with fear;* **but I followed the Lord my God fully.** *So Moses swore on that day, saying, "Surely the land on which your foot has trodden will be an inheritance to you and to your children forever,* **because you have followed the Lord my God fully."**

Caleb was faithful to God because he followed the Lord fully, regardless of what it cost him, or the difficulty of the path God set before him.

I am sure Caleb had a few discouraging days during the forty years of wilderness wanderings. No doubt he, too, grew tired of eating manna. No doubt there were times when he had to wait for God to quench his thirst. He had every opportunity to resent his fellow Israelites as their disobedience and lack of faith were the reasons he had to wait for what God promised. Yet, I also imagine there were many conversations around the campfire as he told the stories of what he'd seen God do, educating the younger generation, bolstering their faith in God, and creating an anticipation of what lay ahead of them if they trusted and obeyed God.

Faith Enacted

Caleb received the "hill country" he asked for, a place of fortified cities and the warriors known as Anakim. He was undeterred by the size of the task. In faith he proclaimed, *perhaps the Lord will be with me, and I will drive them out as the Lord has spoken* (Joshua 14:12). He did exactly that, and the place was renamed Hebron.

Hebron was twenty miles north of Beersheba and twenty miles south of Jerusalem. Beersheba is significant as the place Abraham dwelled after offering Isaac on Mount Moriah. It was Abraham who received the covenant from God concerning the Promised Land, and God will complete that same covenant when Jesus sits on the throne in Jerusalem. Because he followed the Lord fully, Caleb was living right in the middle of God's promises!

One of the most significant characteristics of Caleb's faith is its longevity. He is the ultimate example of a young man who surrendered fully to the Lord early in life and walked with God all the days of his life. Despite the hardships, despite the unfair and difficult things that God allowed to touch his life, his faith in God only grew deeper and stronger. His commitment to take God at His word, to trust in God's power, and rely fully on God's strength allowed him to see many of God's promises fulfilled, even if he had to wait until he was eighty-five!

Give me a faith like Caleb. When I'm old and gray, when my physical strength has diminished, when my mind and body bear the scars of sin and of living in an unfriendly world, may my faith be stronger than ever! As we grow older, let us give testimony to the generation behind us of the goodness and faithfulness of God, both in word and deed. May we be living examples of the power of a life lived fully for God.

Psalm 27:4 – *One thing I have asked from the Lord, that I shall seek: that I may dwell in the house of the Lord all the days of my life, to behold the beauty of the Lord and to meditate in His temple.*

Faith Expressed

Dear Father, Thank You for Caleb's example which inspires us to follow You fully all the days of our lives. May the trials of life make us bolder and more confident in Your goodness, and may we always be willing, like Caleb, to tackle the challenges of life with ultimate confidence in you, no matter how old we are. In Jesus' Name, Amen.

DAY 13: GIVE ME A FAITH LIKE GIDEON

The Lord looked at him and said, "Go in this your strength
and deliver Israel from the hand of Midian. Have I not sent you?"
He said to Him, "O Lord, how shall I deliver Israel? Behold, my family is the
least in Manasseh, and I am the youngest in my father's house."
But the Lord said to him,
"Surely I will be with you, and you shall defeat Midian as one man."
–Judges 6:14-16

Faith Examined

Gideon was an unlikely hero who fought and won a great battle in the most improbable way. The children of Israel had once again chosen evil and turned away from God. Oppressed by the Midianites (a divinely orchestrated discipline), the Israelites were hiding in caves in the hills, while their farms were raided. Gideon's commission and call comes when the angel of the Lord visits him. Our hero is hiding from the enemy, threshing wheat in a winepress.

The angel's greeting immediately reveals the purpose of the Lord's visit. "The Lord is with you, O valiant warrior." Another translation reads, "mighty man of valor." The Hebrew word is *hayil,* meaning "strength, ability, or efficiency." The angel wasn't referring to physical strength, but a God-given strength of character. As the story unfolds, we find Gideon possesses the rare traits of humility, discernment, and an unfailing trust in God that will give him the ability to obey the unusual battleplan God had in mind.

Before Gideon's name is mentioned in this passage, God sends a prophet to the people to call them to repentance. Repentance of our sin always precedes deliverance from the consequences of our sin. Matthew Henry said, "We have reason to hope God is designing mercy for us if we find He is by His grace preparing us for it."

Gideon's first step of obedience, before he could go out and defeat the enemy that plagued his people, was to deal with the idolatry in his own home. The Lord tells him to tear down Baal's altar and the Asherah pole that his father had built. Gideon obeys, but does it secretly in fear of the community backlash. He was afraid, yet he had the courage to act in spite of his fear. When the townspeople realize what he's done, they are ready to kill him; however, his father has the good sense to challenge their ridiculous claim and tells them Baal can defend himself.

Second, Gideon had the discernment to settle his doubts before moving ahead. He asked the angel to confirm it was God's voice who was calling him. He "put out a fleece" twice to reassure himself he was correctly hearing God. When assured that he had clearly heard God, he was committed to completely trust in God's plan, even when it seemed counterintuitive. By the time the battle began, his army was reduced from 32,000 to 300 men holding trumpets and pitchers. And yet, God gained the victory, causing the enemy to destroy themselves. God's plans are not our plans. He often does not make sense to our human thinking, but that is when His glory shines the brightest.

Faith Enacted

Gideon wasn't chosen for his physical strength, but because he possessed a God-given strength of character and spiritual discernment. He was willing to be *sent*. He humbly acknowledged what he lacked. He had no special pedigree or heritage to rely on, nor did he have any kind of ranking. He was the youngest child of an ordinary, non-descript, unnoticed family. What he did have was faith to believe that God would be with him. This gave him the confidence to accept the call to do something for which he felt ill-equipped, which was to lead his people to victory over their enemies.

When we want victory, like Gideon, we must first be willing to get rid of all other gods in our homes and hearts. God will never use us effectively for His Kingdom work if we hold onto personal sin.

We also must be able to overcome any fears or doubts, whether that means seeking confirmation in prayer until God settles our hearts and gives us peace, or praying specifically for an answer that only God can give. Gideon acted even when he was afraid, and he pursued God's heart until he knew without a doubt he was acting in accordance with God's will.

Give me a faith like Gideon. May we repent quickly when God convicts us, and be diligent to keep our lives free from the cultural gods that steal our hearts. May we trust that when God calls us, He also promises to be with us. And may we obey completely in spite of our natural fears or doubts, even when God's plans seem unusual.

Psalm 138:2-3 – *I will bow down toward Your holy temple and give thanks to Your name for Your lovingkindness and Your truth; for You have magnified Your word according to all Your name. On the day I called, You answered me; You made me bold with strength in my soul.*

Faith Expressed

Dear Father, Gideon didn't seek to make a name for himself. You called him out of an ordinary life, a man whom the world would not see as anyone special. Yet, because You were with Him and because he had faith to listen, obey, and follow Your plans, he won a great victory for his people. May we have faith like Gideon to trust that You aren't mistaken in Your call on our lives. May our confidence be in Your presence, and our strength be rooted in who You are, for the glory of Your mighty name. In Jesus' Name, Amen.

DAY 14: GIVE ME A FAITH LIKE BARAK

Then Barak said to her [Deborah], "If you will go with me, then I will go;
but if you will not go with me, I will not go."
–Judges 4:8

Faith Examined

How many times have you been asked to do something that you weren't quite sure you wanted to do, but agreed to participate if you had the support of someone alongside you? I remember a particularly challenging experience when I joined my youth pastor husband on a "ropes course" outing with a group of teenagers. I have little athletic skills and even less inclination to take risks. However, when the guide split us up in groups of two, he placed the shorter, smaller people with the taller, stronger ones. Thus, my partner was one of the strongest and most athletic of the group.

Knowing I had the support of someone who had the insight, skills, experience, and strength I lacked, gave me the confidence to tackle the challenge.

At first read, the verse above in Judges 4:8 sounds like a *lack of faith* on Barak's part, but as we look at the complete story, we see that he simply was making a wise decision. He chose to link his fate with the prophetess, Deborah, trusting that her relationship with and knowledge of God would give him the advantage needed to defeat their enemies.

In those days, women weren't particularly valued for their strength, abilities, or contributions outside of childbearing, marriage, and service to their husbands. Deborah's situation was a bit different, however. She was a respected prophetess and judge who was sought out for her wisdom. The sons of Israel were fully aware that God spoke to her and that she was chosen by God to lead the people during these years of possessing the Promised Land.

God spoke to Deborah with a specific timeline and plan to defeat their current enemies. Jabin, king of Canaan, and his army commander, Sisera, had terrorized and oppressed the people for twenty years. God heard the cries of His people and promised to defeat them. Deborah instructs Barak to pull together an army of ten thousand and go up against Sisera. Barak agrees, but only if Deborah goes with them.

Deborah consents to go, but reminds Barak that the victory will be awarded to a woman. I like Barak's response; he is not concerned with gaining honor. His motivation is simply to lead the people to victory, and he is willing to forgo any glory to ensure the outcome. He knows Deborah's presence will inspire the people and ensure God's favor on the battle.

Barak and Deborah are victorious, just as God promised. Towards the end of the battle, Sisera escapes and is invited to rest in a tent by a woman named Jael. She appears sympathetic to his cause but has an ulterior motive. Exhausted, he falls into a deep sleep, and she takes the opportunity to drive a tent peg through his temple, effectively ending the reign of King Jabin over Israel.

Faith Enacted

Judges 5 contains a victory anthem entitled "The Song of Deborah and Barak," which gives credit for this victory to all three of these unusual warriors. Two women, Deborah and Jael, and Barak, a man who was willing to let the credit go to someone else. Barak's faith was not in himself as a great warrior. Instead, he trusted the spiritual leadership of Deborah because he knew God's hand was upon her. He had faith to surrender his own ego.

Great faith doesn't always mean we get the glory for our spiritual victories. This is an Old Testament story that illustrates the value of the New Testament principles of the body of Christ. As followers of Jesus, we all have different strengths, and sometimes the greatest expression of faith is recognizing we need help from our brothers and sisters in Christ.

Give me a faith like Barak. Let us not seek our own glory. Let us be willing for the honor to go to others. May we be motivated to exercise faith for the good of all of God's people, and less concerned about our natural desire for recognition. Sometimes the greatest step of faith is to move quietly into the background and do what God has called us to do, even if no one else notices.

In the end, after all is said and done, Barak is the one who receives the honor of being listed in the Hebrews 11 hall of fame. Deborah and Jael aren't mentioned. This inclusion tells me that Barak indeed had a faith which is worth emulating. What others perceive as weakness may be the greatest strength of all.

1 Corinthians 12:22-27 (selected) – *It is much truer that the members of the body which seem to be weaker are necessary; and those members of the body we deem less honorable, on these we bestow more abundant honor ... But God has so composed the body, giving more abundant honor to that member which lacked ... Now you are Christ's body; and individually members of it.*

Faith Expressed

Dear Father, There are times when we feel our faith is weak because we need the support of others, but as Jesus said, the tiniest bit of faith, as small as a mustard seed, is enough. Help us not to judge those who seem to receive more honor as having greater faith. Let us be willing to set aside our own egos and desire for recognition so that the greater work for the Kingdom may be accomplished as we work together as the body of Christ. After all, it's not our glory we seek, but Yours. May You receive all the honor and let us have faith to serve in whatever place You ask. In Jesus' Name, Amen.

DAY 15: GIVE ME A FAITH LIKE SAMSON

Then Samson called to the Lord and said, "O Lord God,
please remember me and please strengthen me just this time, O God,
that I may at once be avenged of the Philistines for my two eyes."
–Judges 16:28

Faith Examined

It might seem out of place to include Samson's story in a devotional about faith. Samson's story is very sad, a testimony to a wasted life, a picture of what happens when we take the gift of life that God means to use for His glory and spend it on ourselves. Even so, his story is included in scripture for a reason; his imperfect faith teaches us much about the grace, mercy, and sovereignty of God.

Samson's birth was unusual. The angel of the Lord visited his parents and promised a son would be born. This was exciting news, because up until this time his mother was barren. The child was to be dedicated to the Lord as a Nazarite from before his birth. His mother was given strict instructions not to drink wine or eat any unclean thing while pregnant. *God chose Samson and set him apart for His sovereign purposes from the womb.* Normally, the Nazarite vow was a voluntary act for a specified period of time, when a person would abstain from three things as an act of consecration or dedication. However, Samson was to be a Nazarite from birth to death, by God's own choosing. The Nazarite vow meant he was never to drink wine or anything from the vine, never to cut his hair, and never to go near a dead body.

Samson had a special calling on his life, and he also had a special gift, which was supernatural strength. God's intent was that Samson would use this gift to deliver Israel from the Philistines, but as you read through the story of how he spent his life, you see that instead, Samson used his gift of strength for his own pleasure and glory. He was drawn into relationships with foreign women who worshipped other gods. He lied. He broke the Nazarite vow when he killed a lion and then went back to get honey from it. He demanded a wife like a spoiled child, and his arrogance and temper cost her life. And he foolishly gave away the secret of his strength when he was deceived by a woman.

Samson wasted what God gave him on physical pleasures and pride. He caused the Philistines trouble at times, but he never accomplished what "could have been" if he had instead chosen to use his gifts and influence for God's glory.

Towards the end of his life, we find Samson in prison, the object of mockery and scorn. His eyes are gouged out and his strength is gone. He is a broken man and seemingly forgotten by God.

This was not, however, the end of his story.

Unnoticed by those who held him prisoner, his hair begins to grow back. One day, his tormenters call for him to be bound between two great columns upon which a house rested. The Philistines wanted Samson brought out to amuse themselves; he was the entertainment of the day. Over three thousand men and women filled the house and the roof, including the lords of the Philistines.

We can't know for certain what was going through Samson's mind that day as he listened to the sounds of revelry and mocking, but we do see a glimmer of hope that his heart was repentant at the end and filled with regret for wasting the life God had given him. He asked God for one final moment of supernatural strength to avenge the loss of his eyes. God heard his request, and in grace and mercy, the power of God surged through Samson once again and brought destruction on the enemies of God's people.

Faith Enacted

Samson's story reminds us that no matter how broken we are, no matter how far we've fallen, no matter how wasteful we've been with the gifts and blessings God's given us, there is hope for repentance until the moment we take our last breath. God hears the prayer of faith and repentance, even in our dying moments.

I believe God forgave Samson in that moment. God's calling and choosing are irrevocable (Romans 11:29), and Samson is listed in the great hall of fame chapter of Hebrews 11 as one of God's faithful servants. His life stands as a reminder of how *not* to serve God, but also as a beacon of hope for those who find themselves at the end of a life filled with regret.

If Samson could speak to us, I feel confident he would tell us not to wait until the end of our lives to get over "ourselves" and surrender our lives to God for His glory. But, he would also give us hope if our story mirrors his.

What has God given you? Are you using it for your glory, or His? Give me a faith like Samson, that returns to God in my darkest moments, trusting that He is able to redeem what I've lost, and will welcome me home at the end.

Acts 3:19 – *Therefore repent and return, so that your sins may be wiped away, in order that times of refreshing may come from the presence of the Lord.*

Faith Expressed

Dear Father, We are often like Samson, caught up in our own pleasures and seeking satisfaction in other things instead of using the gifts and blessings You have given us to bring You glory. May we set aside our own desires and live faithfully for You. And if, by chance, we are approaching our death and realize the mistakes we've made, may we not be too proud to ask for Your mercy, and renew our faith in You, even if it's the last thing we do. In Jesus' Name, Amen.

Day 16: Give Me A Faith Like Naomi

Then the women said to Naomi, "Blessed is the Lord who has not left you
without a redeemer today, and may his name become famous in Israel.
May he also be to you a restorer of life and a sustainer of your old age;
for your daughter-in-law, who loves you and is better to you than seven sons,
has given birth to him."
–Ruth 4:14-15

Faith Examined

Everyone appreciates a good love story, and the book of Ruth is one of the best. Chronologically, it fits with the preceding book, Judges, as the events took place during that period of Israel's history. Bible scholar Matthew Henry attributes its authorship to the prophet Samuel, and I love his thoughts on the design and purpose of the book because he rightly discerns that it's not just Ruth's story, but also Naomi's, and has prophetic implications relating to our Kinsman Redeemer, Jesus. According to Henry's commentary, this story is written for two reasons:

First, *to lead to providence, to show us how conversant it is about our private concerns, and to teach us in them all to have an eye to it, acknowledging God in all our ways and in all events that concern us.* And second, *to lead to Christ, who descended from Ruth, and part of whose genealogy concludes the book. In the conversion of Ruth the Moabitess, and the bringing of her into the pedigree of the Messiah, we have a type of the calling of the Gentiles in due time into the fellowship of Christ Jesus our Lord. And let us remember the scene is laid in Bethlehem, the city where our Redeemer was born.*

When reading this short account, it's evident that Ruth is the central figure in the story; however, Ruth's story wouldn't exist without Naomi's. After her husband, Elimelech, passed away, Naomi is left in a strange land with her two sons. They marry two Moabite women (Ruth and Orpah), but after ten years, both sons die, leaving the three women as widows.

Naomi is very sad, bereft of her family and feels that God has dealt bitterly with her. She receives word that the situation has improved in Bethlehem, so she decides to go home. Orpah stays in Moab, but Ruth clings to Naomi, determined not to separate from the mother-in-law she has come to love. Ruth has embraced Naomi's God, and her old life of paganism is no longer an option.

You might know how the story turns out. Ruth shows herself to be a kind, gracious, humble, hard-working, and loving woman. She cares for Naomi like her own mother and goes into the fields to glean so they will have food to eat. God directs her steps into the field belonging to Boaz, and after a few months, Naomi realizes this is God's hand of provision for Ruth.

Naomi instructs Ruth in their customs of levirate marriage. Boaz is a near kinsman and has cultural obligations to take Ruth as his wife and raise up children so that

Elimelech's family line will not die out. Boaz is delighted that this beautiful young woman has come to him and fulfills his duty. Scripture indicates it's just a short time until Ruth conceives and gives birth to a son, Obed, who will be the grandfather of King David.

In our culture, the term "mother-in-law" is often synonymous with an overbearing, ill-willed shrew who torments the woman her son marries, never believing she is good enough. I believe this story reveals a different kind of mother-in-law in Naomi. Even though the two women her sons married were not the ones she would have chosen, she recognized the providence of God had brought this about. By Ruth's response to the idea that she could be separated from Naomi, we can conclude that Naomi fully embraced her, loved her, and taught her about Jehovah, the God of Israel.

Naomi did not have to pursue finding a husband and provider for Ruth, but her faith allowed her to see God's hand of providence in placing Ruth in Boaz's field. She looked out for Ruth's interests, and in the process, God blessed her with a grandson, and her family was included in the Messianic line.

Faith Enacted

Naomi's faith teaches us that when the hand of God allows our lives to go through painful times, we can still trust Him to be faithful. Naomi also teaches us to have faith that God can bring good out of difficult circumstances we wouldn't choose. She loved Ruth in spite of her pagan background and embraced her into the family. She was willing to teach her about her God and invited her into the faith. As a result, she received a blessing she could not have imagined.

Sometimes God puts people in our lives we wouldn't choose. Sometimes God allows circumstances that challenge our belief and hope, and we need faith like Naomi to sustain us until we see the outcome of His providential work for a greater purpose.

Give me a faith like Naomi. Let me love others well, trust God to provide, and be ready to act when He shows me the path of His providence.

1 Samuel 2:7-8 – *The Lord makes poor and rich; He brings low, He also exalts. He raises the poor from the dust, He lifts the needy from the ash heap to make them sit with nobles, and inherit a seat of honor; for the pillars of the earth are the Lord's, and He set the world on them.*

Faith Expressed

Dear Father, I know that You are always at work, and that nothing happens to me without Your permission. I can trust Your providential design for my life. Teach me to have faith like Naomi, faith that sees past any pain You have allowed, and look forward to the blessings You have waiting on the other side. In Jesus' Name, Amen.

Day 17: Give Me A Faith Like Achsah

Then she said, "Give me a blessing;
since you have given me the land of the Negev,
give me also springs of water."
So he gave her the upper springs and the lower springs.
–Joshua 15:19

Faith Examined

Joshua 15 is a historical list of the borders of Judas inheritance in the Promised Land. If you're like me, you find yourself skim reading the names of towns not easily pronounced. Surprisingly, in the middle of the chapter, the narrative breaks to include a story about God's faithful servant, Caleb, and his daughter, Achsah. I've learned that nothing in scripture is random, and when God inserts unexpected details, we ought to stop and take a second look.

After waiting 45 years for God to fulfill His promise to Caleb, he finds himself the new owner of the area called Hebron. He has taken possession, having driven out the previous occupants at God's command, but there's one city remaining, Kiriath-sepher. Perhaps tired of fighting, he declares a challenge: the one who captures this final city will win the hand of his daughter, Achsah, in marriage. Apparently, she was worth the risk, as Othniel, Caleb's nephew, immediately steps up to the plate, takes the city, and wins his prize!

Achsah is a woman ahead of her time. She persuades her new husband to ask her father for her own inheritance. He obliges by giving her the land of the Negev. However, this is not enough for Achsah. She goes personally to visit her father and makes another bold request. She doesn't just want the land; she wants the springs of water that will make it profitable, fertile, and fruitful. She doesn't settle for less than what will make her inheritance truly abundant and meaningful. Caleb obviously loves his daughter; he gives her both the upper and lower springs that surround her inherited land, assuring her success.

I love Achsah's boldness. I appreciate the relationship she had with her father which enabled her to ask for what she needed. And, I love Caleb's fatherly indulgence to not only provide for her immediate need (the land), but to give her something that would bring continued blessing and fruitfulness both in her life, and in the lives of her children and grandchildren to whom she would pass it down.

Faith Enacted

This is a story with obvious physical and literal meaning. Land needs water to produce, and Achsah was a smart woman who anticipated that need. But, I believe there is a greater spiritual lesson for us, especially since it's an unexpected detail God chose to give us. How often do we settle for the physical blessings our Heavenly

Father gives us without giving further thought to the far more valuable spiritual blessings? This story brings us to Jesus' words in John 7:37-39, as he challenges the unbelieving Jews during the celebration of the Feast of Booths.

Now on the last day, the great day of the feast, Jesus stood and cried out, saying, "If anyone is thirsty, let him come to Me and drink. He who believes in Me, as the Scripture said, 'From his innermost being will flow rivers of living water.'" But this He spoke of the Spirit, whom those who believed in Him were to receive; for the Spirit was not yet given, because Jesus was not yet glorified.

As parents, just like Caleb, we want to provide for the physical needs of our children. We want to tuck them safely in bed at night and have ample food in our pantry when they wake up hungry. We want to clothe them warmly, give them good opportunities for education, and watch them grow physically strong as they play.

But Achsah's bold faith teaches us to pursue the greater blessing. We want our children to not only believe in God, but also to experience the abundance of His presence. We want *spiritual life* for both ourselves, and our children. We want God's indwelling Spirit – the true "upper and lower springs" of our promised inheritance in Christ. Through faith in Christ, our loving Heavenly Father not only provides our physical needs, but He also promises to give us Himself – the Spirit of God – who will bring the abundant fruitfulness our souls crave.

Achsah teaches us to have faith that pursues the abundant life Jesus came to give us (John 10:10). It is good to trust God by asking Him to provide for your physical needs, but don't stop there. Pursue your spiritual inheritance. Those who place their faith in Christ are promised the extraordinary, soul-satisfying experience of walking according to the Spirit who indwells all who believe. It is this life alone that is worth passing down to our children. Don't settle for the things of this world only. Have faith like Acshah and ask God for the springs of living water.

Luke 11:13 – *So if you, despite being evil, know how to give good gifts to your children, how much more will your heavenly Father give the Holy Spirit to those who ask Him?"*

Faith Expressed

Dear Father, Thank You for the promised gift of the Holy Spirit, who comes to indwell all who place their faith in Your Son, Jesus. He brings us the abundant life which You desire all of us to experience, as we learn to walk in sync with You. You are the life-giving water for our thirsty souls. Teach us to have faith like Achsah, who did not settle for just the immediate physical needs, but asked her father for a complete inheritance. Thank You for being a good Father, who gives us more than we deserve or need. In Jesus' Name, Amen.

DAY 18: GIVE ME A FAITH LIKE HANNAH

[Hannah] said, "Oh, my lord! As your soul lives, my lord,
I am the woman who stood here beside you, praying to the Lord.
For this boy I prayed, and the Lord has given me my petition which I asked of
Him. So I have also dedicated him to the Lord; as long as he lives he is
dedicated to the Lord." And he worshiped the Lord there.
–1 Samuel 1:26-28

Faith Examined

Everything we know about Hannah is contained in the first two chapters of 1 Samuel. She was married to a man who loved her, but who also had a second wife, Peninnah, a cruel woman who provoked Hannah bitterly, seeing her as a rival for her husband's affections. Peninnah had several sons and daughters, but Hannah was barren, by God's sovereign choice. *The Lord had closed her womb* (1 Samuel 1:6).

As Hannah's story unfolds, we see three critical elements in her faith.

#1 – Hannah had faith to pray persistently and diligently.

Hannah and her husband made an annual journey to Shiloh to offer sacrifices at the place of worship. Year after year, during these times of sacrifice, Hannah prayed diligently that God would grant her the ability to conceive. We see the depths of her pain in the way she prayed; she was *greatly distressed* and *wept bitterly* (1:10). Her heart was focused entirely on God to such a degree that Eli, the priest, thought she might have been drunk as he watched her lips move, but heard no audible sound.

#2 – Hannah had faith to promise God what she knew would be painful.

On this particular year, Hannah makes a vow. If God gives her a child, she will give him back to serve the Lord all the days of his life. I don't believe Hannah made this promise lightly. Having desired a child for so long, she fully understood what it would mean to give him back to God; she also knew God would give her the strength if He answered her prayer.

God hears her prayer and grants her petition. This does not set a precedent to "make deals" with God, but God saw Hannah's heart, and in His sovereign purposes, He honored her request. She conceives and bears a son, whom she names Samuel, meaning "name of God," or "God hears." Each time she pronounced his name, she would be reminded that this child was an answer to her prayers, and that he belonged to God, not her.

#3 – Hannah had faith to fulfill her promise.

For the next few years, Hannah stays at home while her husband makes the yearly trek to Shiloh, savoring the time she has with her son. As a mother, I can only imagine what might have gone through her mind as she put him to bed each evening, knowing that she was one day closer to saying good-bye to him. However, Hannah never wavered in fulfilling the vow she had made to give Samuel in service to God. It would have been easy to delay the parting, to justify another year at home, to find another reason why it was not the best time to surrender her child into the care of Eli and the other priests. But scripture is clear, as soon Samuel was weaned, she took him to the Lord in Shiloh, *although the child was young* (1:24). Without hesitation, though surely her heart grieved, she had faith to honor what she had promised the Lord in gratitude that He had heard and answered her prayers.

We see the core values of Hannah's faith in the song of thanksgiving recorded just after leaving her son in Shiloh: *My heart exults in the Lord...There is no one holy like the Lord, indeed there is no one besides You, nor is there any rock like our God* (1 Samuel 2:1-2). Hannah's faith was grounded not in the things God gave her, but in who God is in Himself. She trusted God because she knew He is good and holy, and deserving of her sacrifice. She had faith that just as God had fulfilled her desire for a child, He would sustain her heart in giving that child back to Him.

Faith Enacted

God honored Hannah's willing faith by giving her three more sons and two daughters. She learned a valuable lesson; God is faithful and trustworthy. When we entrust what is most precious to us to Him, He will give us more than we can imagine.

How about us? Have we prayed faithfully and diligently for what we need or desire? Have we sought God's help, and made promises that we will serve Him in return if He rescues us? Have we asked for His provision, assuring God we will use what He gives us for His Kingdom?

It's easy to forget the promises we made to God in the hard times.

We need faith like Hannah to follow through with our vows even when it's painful or difficult. May we not take His blessings for granted, but freely and generously give all things back into the capable hands of the God who loves us more than we know. He hears the persistent prayers of our hearts, and He is worthy of our trust when He answers.

Psalm 52:8-9 – *But as for me, I am like a green olive tree in the house of God; I trust in the lovingkindness of God forever and ever. I will give You thanks forever, because You have done it, and I will wait on Your name, for it is good, in the presence of Your godly ones.*

Faith Expressed

Dear Father, Thank You for hearing and answering our prayers. Give us faith like Hannah to trust You with the blessings You provide, and find joy in giving them back for Your glory and honor. May we honor our promises, even when it's painful. In Jesus' Name, Amen.

DAY 19: GIVE ME A FAITH LIKE SAMUEL

> Moreover; as for me, far be it from me
> that I should sin against the Lord by ceasing to pray for you;
> but I will instruct you in the good and right way.
> –1 Samuel 12:23

Faith Examined

As I read through the story of Samuel's life, I am amazed at God's grace and sovereignty. Samuel had been dedicated to the Lord's service before he was conceived. He had grown up in the priesthood, and clearly marked as a prophet of God from a young age. His life was completely focused on leading the God's people to worship God, advising them in daily life, judging their quarrels, directing them in times of battle, and speaking God's will and wisdom in all circumstances.

Now, the people have asked for a king so they can be like other nations, essentially rejecting Samuel's leadership and ultimately declaring that God's oversight isn't enough. They want a king they can see. At first read, it seems oddly indulgent for God to give in to their request and choose a king for them, but in fact, His sovereign plan is being fulfilled. He is setting up a kingship, which His own Son will one day fulfill.

Saul seems an unlikely leader; on the day of his coronation, he is hiding among the baggage! A search has to be made for him before they can crown him king. This doesn't hinder God's plan or mean that He has chosen the wrong man; Saul is the perfect candidate because any good thing that Saul does will clearly be by God's hand alone. God's Spirit comes on Saul in ways that are obvious. He begins prophesying, revealing God's power in Him. Samuel tells him, "You will be changed into a different person." God's Spirit comes on him and fills him with righteous anger at the Ammonites who are oppressing the people, and he leads the people in battle.

As Saul takes on the role of king, Samuel, now old and gray, is feeling a little rejected. He gives a parting speech, asking the people if he's done anything wrong during his years of leadership, because if he has, he wants to make it right. He reminds the people again that they have gone against God by asking for a king, yet He has given them what they want. He urges them not to rebel against God and turn again to the idols, so it will go well with them. When the people realize they have crossed a line with God, demanding something that they can't turn back from, they are afraid.

It's in this moment that we see the heart of Samuel's faith. His confidence in God's sovereign plans isn't in the people's ability or inability to obey His commands, but in the covenant-keeping character of the God who calls them out to be His people. Samuel knew that God would accomplish His will and plans through Israel, *despite Israel*. His faith also gave him a correct perspective of his own role in the unfolding history that God was weaving through this rebellious nation – a perspective of humility grounded not in faith in his own leadership, but in the God who had called him to lead.

Faith Enacted

Were it not for his faith in God's sovereignty, Samuel could easily have grown bitter towards the people. Instead, he shows them abundant grace. He assures them *the Lord will not abandon His people on account of His great name* and even though they have effectively rejected him, he promises to pray for them and continue to teach them the way that is good and right (1 Samuel 12:20-25).

There are two lessons in these events that should strengthen our faith in God's sovereignty. First, the people's insistence on selecting a king led them down a path of disobedience, yet it could not derail God's sovereign plans. There are times when God indulges our foolish whims to teach us life lessons and cause us to depend on Him. He lets us experience times when our hearts lead us astray, so that we realize how dependent we are on His mercy and grace. Faith in God's sovereignty will sustain us through the failures of our fleshly desires as we return to Him in repentance.

Second, faith in God's sovereignty is a constant reminder that life is made up of seasons. Like Samuel, there are times when we are called to step up and lead, and other times when we are given the supporting role of praying for and encouraging others to lead. But in all seasons, we trust that God is working out His perfect plans. If we remain faithful to His will and His word, He will empower us and change our hearts to be the person He intends us to be, fulfilling the roles in which He calls us to serve.

Has God blessed you with a position to serve Him? Then serve faithfully, for as long as He allows you to remain in that place of responsibility. But keep your eyes on Jesus, not on the position or role you fill. Your faith is not in the job, and your worth in the Kingdom is not defined by what you accomplish.

Give me a faith like Samuel – a humble faith that is willing to be in the forefront as a leader, and just as content to serve quietly in the background, trusting that God is working out His sovereign plans. May we be Kingdom-minded, but not seek our own kingship. May we extend grace to those who follow, and greater grace to those who may reject us, because our faith rests in the sovereignty of God.

Colossians 3:23-24 – *Whatever you do, do your work heartily, as for the Lord rather than for men, knowing that from the Lord you will receive the reward of the inheritance. It is the Lord Christ whom you serve.*

Faith Expressed

Dear Father, How thankful we are that You are sovereign over all the affairs of our lives. Our failures cannot thwart Your plans. May we have faith like Samuel, to serve You willingly and humbly in whatever role You choose to cast us, as You unfold Your sovereign plans. Let us serve one another with grace, showing mercy when others disappoint us, and keep our eyes fastened on You alone as our Lord and King. In Jesus' Name, Amen.

DAY 20: GIVE ME A FAITH LIKE DAVID

Wait for the Lord and keep His way,
and He will exalt you to inherit the land;
when the wicked are cut off, you will see it.
–Psalm 37:34

Faith Examined

David's story is central to Israel's history. He is the most revered and honored of all their kings, having ruled over the nation during its glory days. There is much to admire about his faith. Even in the worst of failures (murder and adultery), his life is a testimony to God's mercy and grace, and the faithfulness of God to redeem our stories if we remain faithful to Him.

God chose David for one particular reason. *The Lord has sought out for Himself a man after His own heart* (1 Samuel 13:14). This affirmation by God is astounding. What characteristics define a man who is "after God's own heart?"

Man was created in the image of God, having a body, soul, and spirit (1 Thessalonians 5:23). The word used for heart is the Hebrew *lebab*, a noun, meaning the inner man. It describes the soul, the will, and the understanding. The heart is that unseen, immaterial part of a man upon which God does His transforming work. At salvation, God renews our spirit, bringing it to life from a spiritually dead state and enabling us to enter into a relationship with Himself. (Ephesians 2:1-6; John 4:24). His Spirit takes up residence in our spirit, and begins the work of sanctification, or the transformation of our soul (heart) into the image of Christ (2 Corinthians 1:22). Until we receive our immortal, glorified body upon our resurrection from the dead, we live in a state of battle between our unredeemed flesh and the Holy Spirit who lives in us (1 Corinthians 15:50-57).

David understood from personal experience this battle between flesh and spirit. He also knew his faith would rise or fall on the condition of his heart. He became a "man after God own heart" in two distinct ways.

#1 – David's faith was grounded in devotion to God.

1 Kings 11:4 – *For when Solomon was old, his wives turned his heart away after other gods; and his heart was not wholly devoted to the Lord his God as the heart of David his father had been.*

This phrase, "wholly devoted," is also translated "complete, perfect, whole, full." It speaks of keeping a covenant relation. David wasn't perfect; he sinned because he still lived in a fleshly, unredeemed body, but when confronted with his guilt, he immediately confessed, repentant and broken-hearted that he had dishonored the Lord. Faith that is wholly devoted to God's heart leaves no room for hidden places of sin or rebellion. It's a faith that understands we can be at peace with God, completely forgiven and made whole *only* when we have surrendered *every part of our lives* to Him, and our only purpose in life is to follow and pursue Him.

#2 – David's faith was grown in obedience to God.

1 Kings 15:5 – *Because David did what was right in the sight of the Lord, and had not turned aside from anything that He commanded him all the days of his life, except in the case of Uriah the Hittite.*

David understood that being wholly devoted to God was more than an emotional, mental, or spiritual decision. His faith in God expressed itself in the tangible and the practical. He made it his life's goal to do what was right in the sight of God by obeying all of His commandments. He made no excuse for his sin but acknowledged his transgression of God's laws. And according to scripture, he learned from his failures. Having faced the depths of his own fallen and depraved nature, he had no desire to repeat his mistakes. That is the essence of the sanctification of our hearts.

Faith Enacted

David's faith is on display in the Psalms, giving us a front row seat to the transforming power of God's Holy Spirit. Take, for example, Psalm 37. Words like "trust, dwell, delight, commit, rest, and wait" teach us the secrets of his relationship with God. By faith, he understood the sovereignty of God; he had complete confidence in God's goodness and righteousness; and he was willing to wait for God's justice on the wicked and rebellious. He pursued God's heart, being wholly devoted, and lived practically to please God's heart by his willing, daily obedience. As a result, his faith grew deeper and stronger with each passing year.

Give me a faith like David. May my heart be completely consumed with knowing, pursuing, and seeking God's presence. May my will be surrendered to His, and my mind and heart determined to obey His commands in every issue of life. Wouldn't that be a wonderful affirmation upon entering heaven, that God would say of us, "There is a woman or man after My own heart!"

Psalm 119:30-32,57-58 – *I have chosen the faithful way; I have placed Your ordinances before me. I cling to Your testimonies; O Lord, do not put me to shame! I shall run the way of Your commandments, for You will enlarge my heart. ... The Lord is my portion; I have promised to keep Your words. I have sought Your favor with all my heart; be gracious to me according to Your word.*

Faith Expressed

Dear Father, Thank You for pursuing us; may we honor You in return by offering ourselves to You. Grant us a desire to know and obey Your word in all things. Give us a faith like David's. May our hearts be wholly devoted to You, our eyes focused only on You, our ears inclined to listen with intent to obey, and our wills fully bent to the instruction and leading of Your Holy Spirit. In Jesus' Name, Amen.

DAY 21: GIVE ME A FAITH LIKE JEPHTHAH

When he saw her, he tore his clothes and said,
"Alas, my daughter! You have brought me very low,
and you are among those who trouble me;
for I have given my word to the Lord, and I cannot take it back."
–Judges 11:35

Faith Examined

This might be the first time you've heard about Jephthah. His story is recounted in Judges 11-12, and after reading it, you might be surprised to find his name listed in the Hebrews 11 hall of fame next to some pretty famous people – Gideon, David, Samuel, and Samson (Hebrews 11:32). This begs the question, "Who is Jephthah, and how did he reveal an exemplary faith in God?"

Jephthah was the illegitimate son of a prostitute. That fact alone is encouraging; our origins and our past cannot prevent God from making us useful to His Kingdom. Jephthah's father had other sons by his legal wife, and when they all reached adulthood, they cast out Jephthah, fearing he would take part of their inheritance.

Rejection doesn't seem to bother Jephthah. Having a reputation as a "valiant warrior," he goes off on his own and builds a family of "worthless fellows" like himself. This part of his story reminds me of David, whose first army was made up of everyone who was "in distress, in debt, and discontented" (1 Samuel 22:2). Don't you love how God can dramatically change the course of our lives?

After some time, the Ammonites begin to afflict Jephthah's people, the sons of Gilead. They realize they need his help and promise to make him chief over the tribe if he will rescue them. While Jephthah can't resist giving them a bit of a hard time, he agrees to help, and assembles his men to confront their enemy.

Two things happen that reveal the Jephthah's faith. First, as a valiant warrior, we would expect he would immediately take up arms and attack the Ammonites, but instead he shows great restraint and wisdom, as well as a confidence in God as the sovereign ruler over the affairs of men. He sends a message to find out why the Ammonites want to fight.

The Ammonites held the position that Israel had stolen land from their ancestors as they came up from Egypt. Jephthah, however, knew the true history. Israel had requested safe passage promising not to harm either Moab or Ammon as they passed through their land, but this offer of peace had been rejected. Their hostility against God's people resulted in God giving them the territory. Ammon was in the wrong, but refused to acknowledge their part in the animosity between the nations. Jephthah made ready to go up to battle.

Jephthah is most known for what happens next, and it is a source of controversy among Bible scholars. He makes a vow to God to "offer up as a burnt offering" the first thing that comes out of his house if God will give them victory. Obviously, he was expecting a bull, a goat, or a sheep. There was no reason for him to make such a vow; he could have simply asked God to be with them, but like all of us, Jephthah spoke without thinking. He knew he could not win without God's help and wanted assurance of it. God gives Jephthah victory, but upon his return home, he realizes how foolish his vow was, for it is his only daughter who greets him. He has promised God something that will cost him dearly to fulfill.

Faith Enacted

Did Jephthah really sacrifice his only child as a burnt offering? Scripture says he "did according to the vow which he had made" (Judges 11:39), but we must see this statement in context of the rest of the passage, as well as the character and nature of God revealed in all of scripture.

Human sacrifices were strictly forbidden in scripture, and an abomination in God's sight (Leviticus 20:1-5; Jeremiah 7:31; 19:5; 32:35). It is inconceivable that Jephthah would be listed in Hebrews 11 if he had done such a thing in the name of honoring God. The context tells us that his daughter would be given to the service of the Lord, never to marry or bear children. She asked for two months to go with her friends and "weep because of her virginity," and after Jephthah "did according to the vow," she "had no relations with a man." These added details aren't irrelevant. Instead, they tell us how Jephthah fulfilled his foolish vow even though it was painful and changed the course of his daughter's life. It also changed his life, as he would have no heirs and his family line would end.

Jephthah's faith is similar to Hannah's, who also offered her child back to the service of the Lord, although Hannah did it knowingly and intentionally. Faith that results in obedience to God, honoring our vows and promises, and giving up what we think is rightfully owed to us in this life, must be rooted in the character and nature of God. Jephthah learned that God is not a man like us to be bargained with. His faith allowed him to follow through, trusting that God is innately good and righteous. His faith was firmly anchored by his fear and respect for God, who did not take Jepthah's vow lightly.

In what is your faith anchored? Give me a faith like Jephthah, that recognizes God's sovereignty and right to rule over His people and trusts Him enough to keep my promises to Him – even the foolish ones.

Deuteronomy 23:21 – *When you make a vow to the Lord your God, you shall not delay to pay it, for it would be sin in you, and the Lord your God will surely require it of you.*

Faith Expressed

Dear Father, In today's culture, vows are often broken without a second thought, but You hold us to our words and promises. You always keep Your word to us. Give us a faith like Jephthah's to set our roots deeply in Your righteousness and goodness and keep our promises without delay. In Jesus' Name, Amen.

DAY 22: GIVE ME A FAITH LIKE EZRA

Then I proclaimed a fast there at the river of Ahava,
that we might humble ourselves before our God to seek from Him a safe
journey for us, our little ones, and all our possessions.
For I was ashamed to request from the king troops and horsemen
to protect us from the enemy on the way, because we had said to the king,
"The hand of our God is favorably disposed to all those who seek Him,
but His power and His anger are against all those who forsake Him."
So we fasted and sought our God concerning this matter,
and He listened to our entreaty."
–Ezra 8:21-23

Faith Examined

It's one thing to *say* you have faith in God; it's another thing entirely to step out in that faith when the stakes are high. This is especially true when the consequences affect not just you, but others in your care.

Ezra was a Levite, a descendant of the high priest Aaron. His role was that of a scribe. He had set his heart to study the law of the Lord and to practice it, and to teach those statutes and ordinances to his fellow Israelites. Ezra lived in Babylon under the Persian rule of King Artaxerxes, and according to the decree of Cyrus the Great, some of his people had already been allowed to return to Jerusalem to rebuild the Temple. Under Darius' rule, the Temple was completed and dedicated; years later, Ezra was impressed by God to join his people and help establish the teaching that was necessary for them to follow God's ordinances and commands.

Ezra has this testimony: *the good hand of his God was upon him* (Ezra 7:6,9). He knew without a doubt that God had opened the king's heart to grant him favor in returning to Jerusalem. Not only did King Artaxerxes grant his request to go, but he also gave offerings of silver and gold to fund their project and decreed that no Persian tax would be imposed on those who served in the Temple, including the priests, the Levites, the singers, the doorkeepers, or any servants of the house of God. Artaxerxes was a pagan king, but he recognized God's authority over His chosen people. We can assume that he saw some political advantage in granting such support and freedom, but whatever motivated him, the ultimate cause was that God had put it into the king's heart (Ezra 7:27).

Put yourself in Ezra's shoes. You have assured the king that God is on your side, and has blessed your endeavor, and that you are acting on His behalf and command. He has supplied everything you need, and you are ready to go, but then you begin to think about the dangers that could await you on the road ahead. Your journey leads through treacherous paths. You are leading a group of priests carrying great amounts of valuable treasure, a sure invitation to those who would rob and pillage you along the way. Your instinct is to request troop support from the king as an escort to assure your safe arrival.

Ezra surely contemplated asking the king for more help, but realized it would portray God as too weak to finish what He had so obviously started. Not only that, it would also put doubt in the king's mind that perhaps Ezra wasn't as confident in his God as he proclaimed. To appeal to the king for safety would be a tacit admission that God wasn't able to protect them, something Ezra wasn't willing to do.

Ezra put his faith to the test. He placed himself in God's hands, and set out, trusting that God would deliver them safely to Jerusalem.

Faith Enacted

God did indeed deliver Ezra and his company safely to Jerusalem. Why? Because Ezra humbled himself to ask. He prayed and fasted and sought God's heart. When he was sure he was acting according to God's plan, he put his faith into action. He was not willing to let his human instincts keep him from doing what God called him to do or bring shame on God's reputation by communicating doubt in His providence and protection.

Has God called you to do something for Him, but you are paralyzed by your human instinct and fear as you analyze every possible hindrance or risk? Do you have a faith in heart, but not in action?

Ask God for a faith like Ezra. When God moves in your life to put opportunities to serve Him, then trust Him to provide every step of the way. He is a God who finishes what He starts. Like Ezra, if you humble yourself and seek Him, He will be favorably disposed toward you, and His hand will not fail to provide.

Philippians 1:6 – *For I am confident of this very thing, that He who began a good work in you will perfect it until the day of Christ Jesus.*

Faith Expressed

Dear Father, Thank you for Ezra's example of unshakeable faith in You. Help us to look at obstacles, and even dangers, through Your eyes, and not with our limited perspective. Help us to trust in Your providence, not our human instincts. Let us act boldly, stepping out in faith, after we have humbled ourselves and asked for Your direction and wisdom. Let us remember all the ways You have provided in the past and let those memories fuel us to an even greater, bolder faith that acts out loud. In Jesus' Name, Amen.

Day 23: Give Me A Faith Like Nehemiah

When all our enemies heard of it, and all the nations surrounding us saw it, they lost their confidence, for they recognized that this work had been accomplished with the help of our God.
–Nehemiah 6:16

Faith Examined

What are you doing *right now* that requires a steadfast, unwavering faith? What has God put on *your* plate? We all have different levels of responsibility, but if you're a Christ-follower, I'm willing to wager God has you in a place of challenge and spiritual growth even in the day-to-day demands on your time and energy. Whether you're a mother discipling little ones, the CEO of an international business, or anything in between, you have people counting on you and tasks to accomplish. And *because* you're a Christ-follower, all of your responsibilities are ultimately part of your role in God's Kingdom work, even when it seems mundane or unimportant.

And for that reason, you need faith like Nehemiah!

Nehemiah had a position of prestige, serving as cupbearer to King Artaxerxes. As a Jewish refugee, he had access to the most powerful man in the Persian kingdom. He also had a heart that was moved with compassion toward his fellow Jews who were suffering in the aftermath of the Babylonian and Persian occupation of his homeland, Israel. His brother had brought bad news – the people were in distress and reproach because the city walls and gates were broken down and burned. Jerusalem was no longer a picture of God's favor and protection; they had lost hope.

Before Nehemiah acted on the need, he first humbled himself in prayer and fasting to see what God wanted him to do about it. He felt strongly that he should personally get involved, so he asked the king for permission and resources to return to his homeland and rebuild the walls. Favor was granted, and when we pick up our story, the work has progressed almost to completion, but not without challenges. He has enemies who would like to see him fail, and they have noisily and irritatingly made their presence known throughout the project.

When it's clear that Nehemiah is going to be successful in accomplishing what God has given him to do, his detractors press upon him more forcefully. Nehemiah 6 describes attacks that are persistent, personal, and perilous, but Nehemiah perseveres because his faith in God is strong and unwavering.

Nehemiah's faith was not distracted by persistent challenges.

Because Nehemiah was firmly convinced that the work he was doing was *God's work,* he was able to ignore the distractions that would have pulled him away. He had his priorities aligned correctly. We need faith that guides us away from responding to the "tyranny of the urgent" and focuses on the greater, more important task that God has given us to do. This not only requires faith, but wisdom from God to plan our days well and be willing to say no (repeatedly) to lesser things.

50

Nehemiah's faith was not discouraged by personal attacks.

Have you noticed, "Everyone's a critic." In our world of social media and instant knowledge, every decision we make is open to input. Nehemiah's reputation was attacked personally, but in faith, knowing whose approval mattered (God's) and whose didn't (public opinion), he persevered, dismissing his critics. We may not be personally attacked, but we are all susceptible to the criticism of others and we can all fall into the comparison trap. Faith that perseveres keeps its eyes on the gold standard of God's Word, and *only* God's Word. If we are living in obedience to God's commands, listening to the correction and conviction of the Holy Spirit, and confident that we are doing what God has called us to do, by faith we can dismiss our critics and walk forward with courage.

Nehemiah's faith was not deterred by perilous threats.

What will you do if the work God calls you to do places you in physical danger? What if standing firm on God's principles pits you against the governing authorities and at risk for consequences you'd rather avoid? Will your faith stand against the perilous threats of Satan, the enemy of all Christ-followers? The Bible tells us as the day of the Lord approaches, persecution of true believers will increase. We need faith that will endure – faith that is stronger than our fears. Nehemiah experienced the temptation to give into his fears, and as a result would have sinned against God by trusting someone else's advice to save his physical life. Instead, he held firmly to what he knew to be true. His life was in God's hands, and he would rather die being faithful to God than reproach His name and live. Do you have that kind of faith?

Faith Enacted

Persistent challenges. Personal attacks. Perilous threats. Which of these will derail your faith and cause you to abandon the work that God has called you to do? As long as we live on this earth, the work of God will find resistance. It's the nature of our fallen creation, and the reality that our enemy is always looking for an opportunity to discourage a child of God. Don't let him. Ask God for faith like Nehemiah and build that wall.

1 Peter 1:6-7 – *In this you greatly rejoice, even though now for a little while, if necessary, you have been distressed by various trials, so that the proof of your faith, being more precious than gold which is perishable, even though tested by fire, may be found to result in praise and glory and honor at the revelation of Jesus Christ.*

Faith Expressed

Dear Father, We want to accomplish the work that You have given our hands to do. Eternity matters, and we know that in the daily, mundane tasks of our human relationships, jobs, ministries, and projects great and small, You are working out Your Kingdom purposes through Your people. We desire to be faithful servants like Nehemiah. Help us to overcome the obstacles that might cause us to stumble and faithfully build what You've called us to build. In Jesus' Name, Amen.

DAY 24: GIVE ME A FAITH LIKE ESTHER

Go, assemble all the Jews who are found in Susa, and fast for me;
do not eat or drink for three days, night or day.
I and my maidens also will fast in the same way.
And thus I will go in to the king, which is not according to the law;
and if I perish, I perish.
–Esther 4:16

Faith Examined

Imagine you are a young teenager girl living with your uncle who had taken you in after the death of your parents. You are in a foreign land because your people had been taken captive and exiled decades earlier. The religious and moral values that are your inheritance are now observed in a hostile environment. Like many others, you and your uncle have made the best of the situation and live quietly out of the way, practicing your faith and trusting God to take care of you.

One day, a royal edict is published that will turn your world upside down. The king has ordered his soldiers to round up the young virgins in the city. Swept up in this group, you find yourself in the king's harem, essentially held captive for the next year, scrubbed, perfumed, dressed up, and instructed how to appeal to a man's sexual desires. You quickly realize you are being prepared to be brought to the king's bed. If you find favor, you might become the next queen, but if not, you'll have lost your virginity, your family, and your faith in humanity, discarded and rejected by a heathen king's whims.

This is a true story, and it happened to Esther.

We sometimes romanticize Esther's story, but the reality was rather harsh for a young Jewish virgin girl. As it turned out, the king did love Esther more than all the women, and she found favor and kindness with him (Esther 2:17). As her new life unfolded in the palace, Esther had to make several significant decisions on the kind of queen she would be in order to remain faithful to God and her heritage as one of God's chosen people.

#1 – Esther's attitude revealed her faith in God's sovereignty.

Esther quickly gained a reputation among the eunuchs who served the king's harem. Scripture tells us she pleased Hegai, who was in charge of the women; she promptly became his favorite. This tells us a lot about her attitude. She could have been resentful, moody, and angry, refusing to comply and making life miserable for the people who had no part in her current situation. Instead, she must have been kind to those who were only trying to help, showing a maturity and grace. She had faith to believe that if God had allowed this to happen to her, He had a purpose in it.

#2 – Esther's humility revealed her faith in God's authority.

Once she was taken into the harem, Esther was no longer under the authority of her uncle, Mordecai. She could have easily accepted her new Persian life and dismissed any spiritual advice he offered. Instead, she remained humble, listening to his counsel, and seeking his wisdom as she took on her new role. At his suggestion, she kept her Jewish identity a secret. Trusting that Mordecai sought God's wisdom, even after she became queen, *Esther did what Mordecai told her as she had done when under his care* (Esther 2:20). Esther still wanted the biblical authority God had placed in her life, because she had faith to know it was in her best interests. She harbored no grand delusions of being queen; she remained a humble servant of God.

#3 – Esther's courage revealed her faith in God's providence.

It wasn't long before Esther realized the greater purpose God had in raising her to the place of royalty. Once Haman's evil plot is publicized, her role becomes clear. When she hesitates, knowing it could mean her death, Mordecai admonishes her to speak up, reminding her, *who knows whether you have not attained royalty for such a time as this?* (Esther 4:14). Esther risks her life to approach the king, but it is God's providential care that results in Haman's execution, Mordecai's promotion, and the Jews' protection against their enemies. After three days of prayer and fasting, Esther has the courage and boldness she needs. Her faith in God's providence has sustained her on the unusual and terrifying path He allowed her to travel.

Faith Enacted

Has God allowed things to happen in your life that you can't understand? Your faith in Him will determine the outcome. What men mean for evil, God works for good. Esther's story would be very different had she not maintained an unshakeable faith in God's sovereignty over the affairs of men, His authority over earthly governments and people in power, and His providence in what we see as tragic circumstances.

We need a faith like Esther. May we trust God's wisdom more than our own needs for comfort and security. May we have faith in Him to say, "If I perish, I perish," knowing that we have remained faithful to His word and His ways, and that our lives are best spent in submission to His plans.

Proverbs 3:5-6 – *Trust in the Lord with all your heart and do not lean on your own understanding. In all your ways acknowledge Him, and He will make your paths straight.*

Faith Expressed

Dear Father, Thank You for Esther's example. She remained faithful to You in spite of the uncertainty of her circumstances. Others would look at her story and see tragedy, but as we view through the lens of Your sovereignty, authority, and providence, we can rejoice in how You used her to save Your people. No matter what happens to us, as followers of Jesus, we can trust You. In Jesus' Name, Amen.

DAY 25: GIVE ME A FAITH LIKE JOB

> Who among all these does not know
> that the hand of the Lord has done this,
> in whose hand is the life of every living thing.
> –Job 12:9-10

Faith Examined

There was a man in the land of Uz, whose name was Job; and that man was blameless, upright, fearing God and turning away from evil. ... And Job died, an old man and full of days.

These two verses (Job 1:1 and 42:17) are the bookends to one of the most interesting stories of all the Old Testament saints. What happens in between those two verses gives us great insight and understanding as we encounter various trials in our own lives. Job had a unique and personal relationship with God, one that exemplifies a solid faith in His character and the humble attitude of one who saw himself at the mercy of the God he trusted.

This story would not have as much meaning without a look at the kind of man Job was: he was blameless (morally innocent, having integrity, ethically pure; lacking nothing; complete, sound, whole), upright (righteous, correct, straight), and feared God (had a reverential respect and awe of Him). He "eschewed" evil, meaning he turned away, departed, and removed anything in his life that offended God.

Job was also wealthy and successful in material things. He had ten healthy adult children with homes of their own and was rich in flocks and herds. He had the respect of his community, a leader in every way. He was *the greatest of all the men of the east* (Job 1:3). He was so conscious of his faith and relationship with God that he would offer sacrifices for his children *just in case* they accidentally sinned.

God had obviously blessed Job beyond measure. These blessings had not turned Job's heart away in pride, but only moved him into a deeper commitment and faith. He was God's "prize pupil" and God had such confidence in the devotion of Job's heart, He held him out to Satan as the supreme example of faith.

Satan could not resist the challenge, just as God knew would happen. Twice Satan is given permission to bring hardship, pain, and suffering into Job's life, taking his children, his wealth, and his health. Job is left with nothing, scraping boils with a piece of pottery, and encouraged by his wife to curse God and die. *Yet in all of this, he did not blame God, and he did not sin with his lips* (Job 1:22; 2:10). His faith was so strong he was able to embrace the adversity God allowed to touch him, just as eagerly and faithfully as he had accepted the blessings of God.

Job's faith is tested for forty-two chapters as he wrestles with what has happened, defends his own integrity to his friends who believe he must have sinned and brought this upon himself, and cries out to God for understanding. In the end, he is vindicated by God as having spoken what was right concerning God, although he was severely humbled for his insistence on asking why God did what He did.

Faith Enacted

Here are just a few lessons in Job's story to bolster our faith and give us hope in the suffering that inevitably comes to those who follow Jesus.

#1 – No matter how faithful, obedient, or righteous we are, we are not excluded from the possibility of suffering. We must trust that God knows best and will certainly allow things to happen that will deepen and grow our faith.

#2 – God may give Satan some freedom to tempt us and cause us pain, suffering, and loss. The enemy was given power over natural disasters and bodily health, at least in Job's case. We must trust that God has Satan firmly on the leash and will give us grace and faith to endure whatever trials He allows. He will see us through.

#3 – God can handle our questions, but it is possible to sin with our lips and attitudes. We must trust God even when He chooses not to reveal His purposes. We must have faith to keep trusting even when we have no explanation for what is happening.

#4 – Our faith must be built on God's character, not our understanding of His actions. There was no reasonable explanation for Job's pain, yet he never wavered in faith, fully convinced that God had the right and the authority to test him, but was still innately good and righteous.

Has God allowed Satan to touch you? Have you lived faithfully for Him, honoring and obeying Him, yet encountered trials and suffering that you can't understand? You need faith like Job. Perhaps you're one of God's prize pupils. He's refining you like molten gold, and just like Job, you will come out on the other side of the trial fully restored, shining in the very glory of God.

James 1:2-4; 1 Peter 5:8 – *Consider it all joy, my brethren, when you encounter various trials, knowing that the testing of your faith produces endurance. And let endurance have its perfect result, so that you may be perfect and complete, lacking in nothing. ... Be of sober spirit, be on the alert. Your adversary, the devil, prowls around like a roaring lion, seeking someone to devour.*

Faith Expressed

Dear Father, Give us faith like Job, to trust You in the unexplainable, difficult times You allow in our lives. Even if we have lost everything, let us look to You, trusting that You are good. Help us not to sin with our lips, or be arrogant with our questions, but have faith that You will bring good from what the enemy means for evil. In Jesus' Name, Amen.

Day 26: Give Me A Faith Like Isaiah

"Come now, and let us reason together," says the Lord,
"Though your sins are as scarlet, they will be white as snow; though they are red like crimson, they will be like wool. If you consent and obey, you will eat the best of the land; but if you refuse and rebel, you will be devoured by the sword." Truly the mouth of the Lord has spoken.
–Isaiah 1:18-20

Faith Examined

Isaiah is considered one of the "major" prophets, serving as God's messenger to His people in some of the most tumultuous times in Israel's history. Isaiah served as the nation's prophet alongside four kings of Judah (Uzziah, Jotham, Ahaz, and Hezekiah). He had great influence on King Hezekiah and the nation experienced a time of revival and returned to the Lord because of Isaiah's preaching. Ultimately, however, the northern kingdom of Israel was taken into captivity by the Assyrian armies, and the southern kingdom of Judah succumbed to the Babylonians as God disciplined His people.

Isaiah's life produced one of the longer books in the Old Testament, sixty-six chapters. His prophecies contain references to the immediate circumstances Israel experienced during and shortly after Isaiah's lifetime, as well as prophecies concerning the promised Messiah that were fulfilled in Jesus. Not only that, but God also gave Isaiah insights into things that will not be fulfilled until the second coming of Jesus and the thousand-year reign of Christ upon the earth, when all Israel will be saved and restored to the land God promised Abraham.

The Gospels quote more from Isaiah than from any other Old Testament book, especially when affirming Jesus as the fulfillment of the Messianic prophecies. The fact that Jesus often quoted Isaiah shows us his timeless words have application for our lives today. This unique perspective began when Isaiah received a vision of God's throne room.

Isaiah 6:1-4 – *In the year of King Uzziah's death I saw the Lord sitting on a throne, lofty and exalted, with the train of His robe filling the temple. Seraphim stood above Him, each having six wings; with two he covered his face, and with two he covered his feet, and with two he flew. And one called out to another and said, "Holy, Holy, Holy, is the Lord of hosts, the whole earth is full of His glory." And the foundations of the thresholds trembled at the voice of him who called out, while the temple was filling with smoke."*

Upon seeing God in all His glory, Isaiah's immediate response was a recognition of his own sin. He feared for his life, knowing that he was unworthy to be in the presence of such holiness. One of the seraphim (angels) takes a burning coal from the altar, touches it to Isaiah's lips, and declares that his iniquity is taken away and his sin is forgiven – a picture of the redeeming power of Christ's blood that would literally be poured out on that same altar hundreds of years in the future.

The result of Isaiah's cleansing is the pivotal lesson for our faith today. As he gazes on the beauty and glory of the Creator, Isaiah hears the voice of the Lord ring out. "Whom shall I send, and who will go for Us?" There is no other possible response from a man who has seen the Lord high and lifted up. **"Here am I. Send me!"**

Faith Enacted

Isaiah *is* sent – to a stubborn people who have insensitive hearts, dull ears, and dim eyes. God's discipline will fall on the nation as He draws Assyria and Babylon out against His people to perform His purposes. What strikes me, however, is that while Isaiah's prophetic messages are clear and direct concerning the people's sin, his desire and heart for their repentance and restoration is equally evident. God graciously keeps Isaiah's eyes on the bigger picture, the grander perspective, of the eternal fulfillment that will take place thousands of years hence. His vivid descriptions of the restored kingdom gave hope to a people experiencing God's discipline for their rebellion.

Isaiah's faith in God's ultimate goodness, His incomparable righteousness, and His sovereignty over all helps us when we find ourselves under the loving, Fatherly hand of His discipline. Like Isaiah, we need to keep our eyes on the final outcome, when Jesus returns in all His glory and does away with all sin, setting up His physical Kingdom here on earth. A faith that sustains us today keeps its eyes on the promised tomorrow. Yes, *the Lord of hosts will have a day of reckoning; the pride of man will be humbled* and *the Lord alone will be exalted in that day* (Isaiah 2:12,17).

We need faith like Isaiah as we speak truth to a world that has rejected our God. Isaiah said the hard things, holding his people accountable for the idolatry and evil deeds that offended God, but he did not leave them without hope. *Though your sins are as scarlet, they will be as white as snow* (Isaiah 1:18). By faith, we've seen the glory of God with the eyes of our heart just as Isaiah did. We also recognize that we are a sinful people in need of atonement from God's altar.

Give us faith like Isaiah. May our response be, "Send me!" as we humbly and faithfully take the message of eternal life and hope to a world that is destined for God's final judgment.

Isaiah 2:2-3a – *Now it will come about that in the last days the mountain of the house of the Lord will be established as the chief of the mountains, and will be raised above the hills; and all the nations will stream to it. And many peoples will come and say, "Come, let us go up to the mountain of the Lord, to the house of the God of Jacob; that He may teach us concerning His ways and that we may walk in His paths."*

Faith Expressed

Dear Father, How grateful we are for the privilege of telling others about You. Keep our eyes on what is to come. Give us faith like Isaiah to proclaim truth with a humble heart that desires repentance and sees ahead to the glorious future You have planned for those who love You. In Jesus' Name, Amen.

Day 27: Give Me A Faith Like Jeremiah

Before I formed you in the womb I knew you,
and before you were born I consecrated you;
I have appointed you a prophet to the nations.
–Jeremiah 1:5

Faith Examined

Do you ever struggle with your identity or purpose? Those who follow Jesus aren't immune from wondering if we're accomplishing anything valuable in God's Kingdom. Stories like Jeremiah's are a reminder that even when our lives don't turn out well from an earthly perspective, we are valuable and precious to God.

Jeremiah served as God's prophet in the years leading up to the Babylonian captivity. God commissioned him as a prophet not just to Israel, but to all the nations, as he would speak God's judgment against His own people as well as the Gentile nations that surrounded them. Like many of us, Jeremiah doubted his ability to do what God called him to do. He was surely aware of his nation's history of stubborn unwillingness to let go of their idolatry. He knew their spiritual condition; God was calling him to a hard and lonely life. God encouraged Jeremiah in three specific ways that can bolster our own faith as we also strive to obey God and live out the purposes for which He calls us.

#1 - **Don't say you're too young** (Jeremiah 1:6-8). Age was irrelevant, because Jeremiah was simply the messenger, the vessel. God promised to be with him and deliver him from those who would oppose him. We might feel too young or too old, but excuses based on our season of life aren't valid if God clearly commands us to do something. Just as He did for Jeremiah, He will be with us and do the work through us.

#2 – **Don't worry about what to say, but say what I tell you to say** (Jeremiah 1:9-12). God put *His* words in Jeremiah's mouth. He told Jeremiah, "I am watching over My word to perform it." The power wasn't in Jeremiah's speaking ability, but in the God who gave him the words. It is God who accomplishes the work; our part is simply to be faithful and obey.

#3 - **Don't be afraid** (Jeremiah 1:8,17-19). God promised Jeremiah He would be with him and would *deliver* him, a sign that the path of obedience would surely lead him through some precarious, uncomfortable situations. Yet he was not to let fear prevent God's word from being proclaimed, *for I am with you.* The antidote to fear is an awareness of God's presence. Knowing He is with us, we are able to obey what He calls us to do.

Jeremiah spends the rest of his life preaching repentance to a people who refuse to listen. After the Babylonians carry off the captives, he is left with the few remaining remnants who are placed under Babylonian authority in their own land. Desperate to escape, the people come to him once more asking for God's advice. They promise to obey whatever God decides. After ten days, the word of the Lord comes to Jeremiah, instructing them to remain in the land as captives and not be afraid. God wants them to trust Him to provide deliverance and provision (Jeremiah 42).

Jeremiah is not surprised when they reject God's counsel and flee to Egypt, where God has clearly warned they will die by the sword as the Babylonian empire advances. Against his will, he is forced to go with this rebellious group. The Bible's account of Jeremiah's life ends here, but church history indicates his own people stoned him. Perhaps in that pagan culture, the exiled Hebrews lost all respect for a prophet of God and finally decided to get rid of him for speaking against their sin. History also tells us that Babylon did invade Egypt shortly after this; God kept His word.

Faith Enacted

From one perspective, Jeremiah's life was a failure. Despite his preaching, in the end, the nation was scattered, the temple destroyed, and the land lay desolate for seventy years. His life's goal was to turn the people back to God. He worked tirelessly and faithfully, but it never happened. What we forget is that history was written from the perspective of the nation as a whole, but we have no idea of the impact Jeremiah made on individual lives. I'm quite sure there were many men and women who made different personal choices, who responded to the conviction of sin and followed God in the face of a resistant culture. Men like Daniel, Shadrach, Meshach, and Abednego, who went into exile in Babylon with a desire to follow God wholeheartedly or others who were part of the remnant and were forced, like Jeremiah, to go to Egypt against their will.

Jeremiah's ministry is still impacting the world today. His life of faith and obedience left a record of the character and holiness of God. Studying his life causes us to examine our own hearts for idols, and grow in our faith and obedience, all because a lonely prophet of God willingly stood against the tide of ungodliness and sinful rebellion that he saw all around him.

We can't know how or when our lives will end. We might not think we're making a difference; and we might believe that no one will remember us when we're gone. From an earthly perspective, our lives can seem wasted and unfulfilled even when we walk in obedience to God's leading. We have to see life from God's perspective with the eyes of faith. Like Jeremiah, we must determine to stand firm, trusting the outcome to God.

Philippians 2:13 – *For it is God who is at work in you, both to will and to work for His good pleasure.*

Faith Expressed

Dear Father, Thank You for calling us to Your Kingdom purposes, even from our mother's womb. You have a plan for our lives that will bring You glory and further Your kingdom. Give us faith like Jeremiah, to see it through to the end, no matter the outcome. By faith we know that You will accomplish Your word. In Jesus' Name, Amen.

DAY 28: GIVE ME A FAITH LIKE EZEKIEL

Therefore, being always of good courage,
and knowing that while we are at home in the body
we are absent from the Lord—
for we walk by faith, not by sight.
–2 Corinthians 5:6-7

Faith Examined

Has God ever asked you to endure something which on the surface seemed cruel or without purpose? As I think about possible answers to that question, the first thought that comes to mind is the untimely passing of a loved one. Death is always difficult to bear no matter how old a person might be, but it seems especially unfair when God takes a loved one at a young age or in the prime of life.

In Ezekiel 24, God asks a very great sacrifice of his faithful prophet. He tells Ezekiel that his wife is going to die; in fact, He says clearly, "I am about to take from you the desire of your eyes with a blow." His wife's death was going to serve God's purpose. God told Ezekiel to respond in a very strange way. Instead of grieving her death, he was to put on garments of celebration (*bind on your turban and put your shoes on your feet*). And so, it is fulfilled, just as God said. Ezekiel's wife dies the very same day he receives this news. In faith, trusting God's sovereign purposes, he obeys and does as God commanded.

Ezekiel's contemporaries were confused by his unusual response, but they knew Ezekiel was God's prophet. They recognized immediately that his actions had meaning for them – that God was sending them a message through Ezekiel's pain.

God's purpose was a lesson for the exiles in Babylon, revealing the hardness of their hearts. He reveals to Ezekiel that He is preparing to take something from them that was their pride and joy and the delight of their souls, the Temple. Nebuchadnezzar has already laid siege to the city of Jerusalem and in just a few short years, he will destroy this beautiful building, the center of their worship. But instead of mourning its loss, God says the exiles will not even blink. They will go on in their iniquities and complain about their captivity. The loss of something precious, something that represents their relationship to God, will not move their hearts. Ezekiel's wife's death, and his abstinence from mourning is a sign of what will happen. Of course, the people don't believe it, but it will happen just as God said. *When it comes, then you will know that I am the Lord* (Ezekiel 24:24).

From God's perspective, and we would believe from Ezekiel's perspective as well, death was not an end, but a graduation into the presence of God. It was areward. It was the ultimate victory. But, it is also a reminder of sin...the sin of Adam & Eve that brought death into the world, and our own sin which sends us to eternal spiritual death away from God in the pain and torment of hell. It is a reminder that we face a battle we can never win in our own strength or our own good works. It is the visible, tangible "elephant in the room" that the atheist, the agnostic, and the apostate can't get around. Death comes for us all, and only God can rescue us from it.

Our circumstances are a bit different from Ezekiel's. We are not in physical captivity, awaiting God's judgment through a conquering nation, yet the death of our loved ones is just as much a warning to those who rebel against God today. Death is a reminder that *it is appointed for man to die once, and after this comes judgment* (Hebrews 9:27).

Faith Enacted

Serving God often means we must be willing to give up something we love in obedience to His higher and greater purposes. Ezekiel was able to obey God and release his wife into God's care without mourning her death because he would meet her again. The opportunity for his people to repent and recognize God was far more important; the issue of physical death had been settled by his faith in God, so it was not too great a sacrifice.

What is your response when God takes something precious from you? Do you have faith to believe that it is for a greater purpose? Do you hold the things that are dearest to you with open hands, trusting by faith that God can only do good, and that His desire is that we find complete dependence, satisfaction and joy only in Him? Are you able to rejoice even in the death of a loved one, as a testimony of your faith and trust in God?

Our response to death is a living illustration to the rebellious world. Give me a faith like Ezekiel. By faith, we rejoice in the hope of heaven for all who have put their trust in Jesus Christ for the forgiveness of sin. May our faithful response be a light that points the way to salvation for all who will heed God's call.

Psalm 116:15 – *Precious in the sight of the Lord is the death of His godly ones.*

Romans 8:28 – *And we know that God causes all things to work together for good to those who love God, to those who are called according to His purpose.*

Faith Expressed

Dear Father, By faith we understand that life and death is in Your hands. We believe that all things come to us by Your hand, and that You are trustworthy and good, even when Your purposes require great sacrifice. Give us faith like Ezekiel, to entrust into Your care even those who are most dear to us. Thank you for the hope of life after death that is available to all who put their faith in Jesus. It is this confident hope that will strengthen us with Your peace and help us be aware of Your presence, even in our darkest moments, and for that we are grateful. In Jesus' Name, Amen.

DAY 29: GIVE ME A FAITH LIKE DANIEL

Then Daniel went to his house and informed his friends,
Hananiah, Mishael and Azariah, about the matter, so that they might request
compassion from the God of heaven concerning this mystery.
–Daniel 2:17-18b

Faith Examined

In his book, *The Knowledge of the Holy,* A.W. Tozer confronts us with this premise: "What comes into our minds when we think about God is the most important thing about us." There's no greater example of this than the young Hebrew, Daniel, who was taken into captivity by Nebuchadnezzar and carried to Babylon to serve the king.

Daniel had a lot of things to be proud of. He is described as one of the sons of Israel who were good-looking, highly intelligent, endowed with understanding and discernment, with a keen ability to learn. I'm sure he was sought after by many families looking to arrange a good marriage for their daughters! Babylon had other ideas. They desired to take the God-given talents and giftedness of these young men and mold them into the pagan culture for their own use. Their plan was simple – a three-year course of indoctrination through education in the literature, language and customs of Babylon.

This plan had two possible outcomes, much like the current college education system of western civilization. They could survive the intentional (re)programming of their values and beliefs and remain faithful to the biblical truth they had been taught from childhood, or their faith would be dismantled, and they would become, for all intents and purposes, children of Babylon. The latter was the desire of the king's heart, and he spared no expense nor missed any detail in their training, even down to the food they ate, as he instructed them to be given the rich meats and wines of Babylon.

What came into Daniel's mind when he thought about God was the deciding factor during his life. If you have read his stories, you already know he is a shining example of a faith that was grounded in a right view of God.

Daniel's faith was tested and proven genuine many times. As his story unfolds, we see three foundational beliefs that testify to a correct understanding of God's character and nature.

God's provision sustains me.
The first challenge to Daniel's faith was a physical one. He had grown up following the strict dietary requirements God had given to the Jewish people. Certain things were unclean, and food had to be prepared under strict rules. From the first meal offered, *Daniel made up his mind that he would not defile himself with the king's choice food* (Daniel 1:8). Wisely, he did not stage a sit-in protest and refuse to eat. Daniel knew God's diet was better for his body, and that God's provision would sustain him, so he respectfully asked the officials for a ten-day trial period during which he and his friends would eat what God had prescribed. Not only were they satisfied and

well-fed, but their appearance was also better than the youths who ate the king's food.

God's knowledge informs me.
Nebuchadnezzar's first dream disturbed him greatly, so he called on his wise men to interpret. Whether he had forgotten the dream or was simply testing the validity of his wise men's professed abilities, he demands they not only interpret the dream, but recount the details of it without his help. Of course, they can't. Frustrated, the king indignantly demands all the wise men to be killed. When Daniel hears the news, he does not panic. He respectfully asks the king for a bit of time, and immediately calls his friends to pray *to the God of heaven* concerning the mystery. Daniel knows if the answer is to be revealed, it will be by divine knowledge, not his. God is faithful to answer his prayers, and when he speaks to the king, Daniel reminds him, *neither wise men, conjurers, magicians nor diviners are able to declare it to the king ... **however, there is a God in heaven who reveals mysteries*** (Daniel 2:27-28a). The knowledge of God is greater, and by faith, Daniel staked his life on that belief.

God's presence protects me.
Both Daniel and his friends experienced the protective power of God's presence. When faced with a choice to worship Nebuchadnezzar or worship *the God in heaven*, Shadrach, Meshach, and Abednego chose certain death over compromise, but God's presence appeared with them in the fiery furnace. Years later, having been promoted over his peers under Darius' rule, Daniel found himself in a quandary. He could remain faithful to his spiritual walk and continue seeking God's presence in prayer as was his daily custom, trusting God's protection. Or he could hide in fear of man and withdraw in secret, hiding his relationship with God in deference to a pagan king. Daniel chose rightly, and God shut the lions' mouths. Darius learned **there is a God in heaven** – the living and enduring God whose kingdom will not be destroyed and whose dominion will be forever (Daniel 6:26).

Faith Enacted

What comes into your mind when you think about God? Anything other than a right view – His true nature and character as revealed in the Word of God – is idolatry and is not the kind of faith that will sustain you when you face your lions. Give me a faith like Daniel. Let me rely on God's provision, trusting His ways are good and right. Let me seek knowledge from Him alone, and cast aside any idea, concept, or belief that raises itself up against the knowledge of God. Let me pursue God's presence daily regardless of the cost to my life, trusting that He will protect me and see me safely home. *There is a God in heaven,* and He is the only God worthy of our faith.

Daniel 2:19b-20 – *Then Daniel blessed the God of heaven; Daniel said, "Let the name of God be blessed forever and ever, for wisdom and power belong to Him."*

Faith Expressed

Dear Father, How grateful we are that You are the God of heaven. May our faith be rooted in a right view of You, for wisdom and power and glory and honor belong to You, and You alone are worthy of our faith. In Jesus' Name, Amen.

DAY 30: GIVE ME A FAITH LIKE HOSEA

Whoever is wise, let him understand these things; whoever is discerning, let him know them. For the ways of the Lord are right, and the righteous will walk in them, but transgressors will stumble in them.
–Hosea 14:9

Faith Examined

Hosea prophesied during the final twenty-five years of Israel's history before the Assyrian captivity. God used Hosea as a living example of the relationship between God and His chosen people by instructing him to marry an unfaithful wife. Gomer was a prostitute, just as Israel had prostituted themselves with the Baals and other false gods. Through Hosea's faithful obedience to His command, God made His point clear. He loved Israel, and desired to care for her as a loving husband, but she would have none of it. She committed spiritual adultery just as surely as Gomer was a physical adulteress. God's heart was broken, and He was also angry at her sin.

Hosea has three children named by God: Jezreel ("God sows"), Lo-ruhamah ("not loved"), and Lo-ammi, ("not my people"). Their names tell the story of what is going to happen. Israel has sown to the wind and will reap the whirlwind as they suffer for a time as an unloved people rejected by their God. The good news is that Hosea also prophesies their restoration. After she has been punished, God promises Israel that in the last days, He will put an end to wars, and "betroth you to Me forever...in lovingkindness and in compassion" (2:18-19). He will "sow her for Myself in the land," and will "have compassion on her who had not obtained compassion," and "will say to those who were not My people, You are My people!" (2:23) Just as Hosea is told to buy back his wife, God will redeem His covenant people (3:1-5).

Hosea's faith is put on display as he advises and admonishes the people. God gives him the words, but it is his sure confidence in those words of truth and his willingness to proclaim them that defines him as a prophet. We can know truth, but if we fail to obey it ourselves and speak it boldly, it does not bear the fruit of faith.

Unfaithfulness to God doesn't happen all at once. As we see in Hosea's message, it is a process that begins in the mind, moves to the heart, and is revealed in our actions.

Israel's minds rejected the knowledge of God.
Hosea 4:1,6a – *Listen to the word of the Lord, O sons of Israel, for the Lord has a case against the inhabitants of the land, because there is no faithfulness or kindness or knowledge of God in the land. ... My people are destroyed for lack of knowledge.*

Israel's hearts replaced their devotion to God.
Hosea 4:12-13 – *My people consult their wooden idol, and their diviner's wand informs them; for a spirit of harlotry has led them astray, and they have played the harlot, departing from their God. They offer sacrifices on the tops of mountains and burn*

incense on the hills ... therefore your daughters play the harlot and your brides commit adultery.

Israel's actions rebelled against God's law.
Hosea 4:2 – *There is swearing, deception, murder, stealing, and adultery. They employ violence, so that bloodshed follows bloodshed.*

We too, can be spiritual adulterers and reap what we've sown. We can reject the knowledge of God, substituting our own ideas. Our hearts will follow, replacing devotion to God with devotion to worldly things. Soon, we will justify sin we know is offensive to God. Because of our sin, we won't feel God's compassion and love. In the end, we no longer delight in being His people. We stay away from church. We neglect our Bibles. We don't pray anymore. Spiritual adultery is the natural result of a divided and unfaithful heart. Hosea saw it in his people, and it is the same path many find themselves on today.

Faith Enacted

Hosea had faith that God could and would redeem His people because He never abandons His covenant. The answer was simple: *Return to the Lord...that we may live before Him...let us press on to know the Lord.* (6:1-3). *It is time to seek the Lord* (10:12).

Hosea's faith was in God's covenant promises. What he witnessed in Israel only affirmed what he knew to be true – *the ways of the Lord are right* (14:9).

God longs to restore us when our hearts, minds, and actions betray the One who loved us and brought us into a covenant relationship with Him through Jesus Christ. When we cry out in repentance, He pulls us out of the pit of destruction and plants us on a firm foundation (Psalm 40:2). He is compassionate and gracious, slow to anger, and abounding in lovingkindness and truth (Exodus 34:6), and longs to show us compassion (Isaiah 30:18). He will never forget His covenant people or break His covenant of love and salvation, even though He may discipline us for a time. We, too, are His chosen people (1 Peter 2:9).

Give me a faith like Hosea, that trusts Him to fulfill the covenant He made at the cross. May we prove faithful as well, as we pursue the knowledge of God, remain devoted to Him, and submit every action in obedience to His commands.

Hosea 3:5 – *Afterward the sons of Israel will return and seek the Lord their God and David their king; and they will come trembling to the Lord and to His goodness in the last days.*

Faith Expressed

Dear Father, We don't want to be spiritual adulterers. We need faith like Hosea, firmly convinced that Your ways are right and good, and that pursuing You is the wise and discerning path. When we do fail, help us to be quick to repent and return. Thank You for the covenant You made with Jesus to redeem us as Your people. In Jesus' Name, Amen.

DAY 31: GIVE ME A FAITH LIKE JOSIAH

Before [Josiah] there was no king like him who turned to the Lord
with all his heart and with all his soul and with all his might,
according to the law of Moses; nor did any like him arise after him.
–2 Kings 23:25

Faith Examined

What does it take for a nation to turn back to God? According to Josiah, it starts in the heart of a person who is determined to walk in the ways of God.

Josiah was only eight years old when he came to the throne. By the time he was sixteen, he had the discernment not to follow his father and grandfather's example, but to seek the God of his ancestor, David. He realized his legacy as king was dependent on who he chose to follow. Both 2 Kings 22-24 and 2 Chronicles 34-35 tell the story. Josiah's determination to follow God with his whole heart, combined with the prophet Jeremiah's powerful preaching to the nation, resulted in a revival that had not been seen since the days of Samuel.

At age twenty, Josiah begins tearing down the altars to the false gods of Baal that have spread across the country. It's a start, but God has more in mind. Six years later, the king has given orders to repair the temple. During the reconstruction and clean-up, a copy of the Torah, the Law of Moses, is found. The priests had evidently discarded it, no longer leading the people in the worship and teaching God had prescribed for His people.

When the scroll is brought to Josiah, he asks his scribe to read it aloud. As he realizes how far his people have strayed from God's Word, his heart is broken. He tears his clothes in repentance and sends the priests and scribes to go and inquire of the Lord for what they should do. He understands his people are suffering under the wrath of God because they have abandoned Him.

Josiah realizes God's Word has to bring repentance and revival; he experienced it in his own heart. He calls the people together to meet at the temple, from the least to the greatest, and stands and reads **all** the words of the Covenant. In public, he pledges himself to *follow the Lord and keep His commands, statutes and decrees with all his heart and all his soul, and to obey the words of the covenant written in this book* (2 Kings 23:3, 2 Chron. 34:31-32). Following the example of their king, the people also enter into the renewed covenant with God.

Revival has come to the nation!

Josiah doesn't simply make a "profession of faith" to follow the Lord and then go back to his palace and his comfortable life. He goes on a mission to destroy every last vestige of idol worship and offensive practice throughout the land. Here are some of the words that describe the action he took on every element of ungodliness: *removed* it, burned it, did away with it, ground it to powder, scattered it, broke down, desecrated so no one could use it, pulled down, threw out the rubble, cut down, got rid of (2 Kings 23). He took decisive, intentional and thorough action that allowed no return to the old ways. He removed **all** the detestable idols from **all** the territory. A complete renewal. A complete repentance. Afterwards, around the restored center of worship, the temple, the nation celebrated the Passover and the Feast of Unleavened Bread as it had not been celebrated since the days of Samuel.

Faith Enacted

Believing by faith that God was true to His Word, Josiah took five specific steps to bring revival to his people.

He repented of his own personal sin and the sins of the nation.
He read God's Word personally and publicly.
He renewed his commitment to obey God's commands.
He removed every false idol and opportunity to sin.
He returned to worshipping God.

What would happen if we had faith to attack the lingering sin and ungodliness in our lives with the same attention and determination as Josiah? What if we had faith to completely eradicate anything that tempts our hearts away from God, that stirs up our mind and heart to think of things other than Him and His glory? If we want to experience real worship, if we want to truly follow Jesus, then nothing less than faith like Josiah's is demanded of us.

How important is God's word to you? Does it wake in you a fiery commitment to follow God wholly and fiercely? Does it stir your heart to long for a complete giving up of yourself to Him? It should. If we read it, study it, believe it, and put its truths into action, we will be Josiah's in our generation. What a difference that would make for our world today. Give me a faith like that.

2 Kings 22:19 – "*Because your heart was tender and you humbled yourself before the Lord ... and you have torn your clothes and wept before Me, I truly have heard you,*" declares the Lord.

Faith Expressed

Dear Father, It takes faith like Josiah's to move beyond mere words of commitment to turning our lives upside down in obedience to Your commands. We can't serve You with a half-hearted faith and expect Your full blessing. Give us faith like Josiah, to determine to seek Your ways, turning neither to the left nor the right. May we have the spiritual strength to eradicate all that displeases You, and live faithfully according to Your Word. In Jesus' Name, Amen.

DAY 32: GIVE ME A FAITH LIKE ELIJAH

The effective prayer of a righteous man can accomplish much.
Elijah was a man with a nature like ours,
and he prayed earnestly that it would not rain,
and it did not rain on the earth for three years and six months.
–James 5:16b-17

Faith Examined

Elijah enters the biblical narrative without fanfare or introduction. We're not given any details on how God called him as a prophet to the kings of Israel. His name means "The Lord (Jehovah) is my God." We don't know if this was the name his mother gave him, or if, by faith, he took up this name for himself as he stepped into the prophetic work to which he was called, but he certainly fulfilled its meaning.

Elijah is one of the most well-known and revered prophets. He was the fiery prophet who stood on Mount Carmel and faced four hundred and fifty prophets of Baal in a memorable stand-off. I've been to that very place in Israel and stood on that mountain, overlooking the Jezreel Valley. It is an inspiring and beautiful place, especially when you are there with other believers, reading this story where it happened, and contemplating the mighty power and faithfulness of God.

We would all love to have the kind of faith it took for Elijah to challenge the prophets of Baal in such a public, life-threatening way. He certainly knew he was putting God "on the spot" and if He chose not to come through, it would be the last challenge of his life. That kind of faith and spiritual maturity doesn't happen overnight. As we read the scripture passages about Elijah's ministry (1 Kings 17-22), we see that "big faith" is built over a lifetime of obedient faith in the small things.

God caused a famine in the land during which time He sent Elijah out into the desert to live by a brook. Elijah didn't stockpile food and make a contingency plan; he obeyed, *an act of faith*. God told the ravens to bring him bread and meat, and he drank from the brook until it dried up and God gave him his next assignment.

God sent Elijah to Zarephath to stay with a widow. The widow had just enough flour and oil to make a cake for her and her son, and then she planned to die. Elijah didn't decide God had made a mistake and look for a richer benefactor. He simply asked her to make the cake for him instead. She generously agreed, *an act of faith*. God performed a miracle, and the oil and flour fed her family and Elijah for the duration of the famine.

This same widow's son became ill and died. Elijah didn't call for the mourners. Instead, he asked to take the child's body upstairs so he could pray over him, *an act of faith* that God could intervene. She could have said "you're crazy" and buried him like one would expect. Instead, in *an act of faith,* she surrendered her son's body into Elijah's care. God answered Elijah's prayers and raised the boy from the dead.

Elijah met Obadiah, Ahab's palace administrator, and asked him to arrange a meeting with Ahab, *an act of faith* that Ahab wouldn't take his life. After all, Elijah was the one who had prophesied the famine that was destroying the kingdom. Obadiah was a devout believer in the Lord, but he knew God had a habit of carrying Elijah off by the Spirit at a moment's notice; he feared Elijah wouldn't appear as promised, causing his own life to be in danger from Ahab's anger. As *an act of faith*, he took Elijah at his word as a man of God and set up the meeting.

It's only after these experiences that we come to Mount Carmel. Elijah wasn't afraid to step out in obedience in a big way that could cost him his life, because he had already seen God's faithfulness in many small acts of obedience, both his own, and others who believed.

Faith Enacted

Do you want to see God do amazing things in your life?
Do you want to be ready when God asks you to obey in the big things?

Start with small acts of obedience, and your faith will grow. Faith always demands obedience, even when it's not logical to our human understanding. God is true to His Word, and He is always faithful to show up when we put our trust in Him and obey.

We could say that Elijah's faith was "out of this world," for when it came his time to lay down the mantle of prophetic work and graduate to his heavenly reward, God arranged a spectacular exit. He didn't simply close his eyes and pass away. As he walked with his young protégé Elisha, *there appeared a chariot of fire and horses of fire ... and Elijah went up by a whirlwind to heaven* (2 Kings 2:11).

Elijah's faith became sight. After a lifetime of seeing God do miracles in response to his obedient faith, it was the most natural thing to step into a heavenly chariot and be borne away into the presence of God.

When our work on earth is done, most likely we won't go up in the whirlwind, but *we will go up*. As our final act of earthly obedience, by faith, our spirit will answer the Holy Spirit's call and in the blink of an eye, we'll be home. Give me a faith like that.

1 Kings 18:36 – *At the time of the offering of the evening sacrifice, Elijah the prophet came near and said, "O Lord, the God of Abraham, Isaac and Israel, today let it be known that You are God in Israel and that I am Your servant and I have done all these things at Your word.*

Faith Expressed

Dear Father, As followers of Jesus, we all want to be remembered as people of great faith, but so often we don't want to obey You in the small things. Teach us to live every day by faith in You. Help us to pay attention when You speak, to listen and obey by faith. We don't need fame or to have our names remembered. May our lives be made up of a lifetime of simple, obedient faith that proclaims, like Elijah, Jehovah is our God! In Jesus' Name, Amen.

DAY 33: GIVE ME A FAITH LIKE ELISHA

> When they had crossed over, Elijah said to Elisha,
> "Ask what I shall do for you before I am taken from you."
> And Elisha said, "Please, let a double portion of your spirit be upon me."
> –2 Kings 2:9

Faith Examined

Unlike Elijah, who appears in the pages of scripture suddenly without introduction, Elisha has a backstory. His story intersects with Elijah at a time when Elijah needed encouragement. After destroying the prophets of Baal, Elijah hears that Jezebel seeks to kill him. Elijah is human, and as often happens after a great spiritual victory, he encounters his own personal spiritual battle of fear. God speaks to him in the still small voice of a gentle breeze, assuring him that he is not alone. In fact, God has selected a young man for him to mentor as his replacement when his work is done.

Elijah sets out to recruit Elisha, the son of Shaphat. He finds him plowing a field with twelve pairs of oxen. Elijah takes his mantle (his robe or cloak) and throws it over Elisha. This was a cultural sign that Elisha immediately understood. He had been selected to be a prophet. The robe represented the Holy Spirit that empowered the prophet to hear and speak the words of God and perform miracles.

Elisha showed great faith in leaving his home and his livelihood to become a prophet. Prophets weren't popular. They were often ridiculed as they spoke words of warning and judgment to a stubborn and rebellious people. Elisha knew what this new life would be like and he did something that speaks volumes about his faith. He takes the pair of oxen who represented his old life and offers them as a sacrifice. He destroyed his back-up plan, signifying he was "all in" for the life to which God had called him.

For several years, Elijah walked *with* Elisha, teaching him by word and example what faith in God looks like. When it was time for Elijah to leave, he asked Elisha what he could do for him. Elisha requested a "double portion of his spirit." While I'm sure Elisha wanted to pattern his ministry after his teacher, having observed his boldness and tenacity in the face of hostile kings, I think he was asking for more than just to "be like Elijah." He knew the power of Elijah's ministry did not rest in Elijah's abilities and personality but was wholly due to the power of the Spirit of God. Having seen what God could do through an obedient servant, Elisha wanted that same power in his ministry, and more of it. He wanted to know God and experience God in even greater ways. And he got his request!

As Elisha watched the chariot of fire transport Elijah to heaven, Elijah's cloak fell to the ground. Elisha *literally* took up the mantle of Elijah and parted the waters of the Jordan. The Spirit of the God of Elijah now rested on him.

Elisha served as God's prophet for sixty years, more than double the length of Elijah's ministry. Two stories illustrate the extraordinary ability of God's Holy Spirit who worked through Elisha as he faithfully served God. From Elisha's perspective, these events weren't unbelievable or even surprising; he had seen and experienced the might and power of God. In fact, miracles are *but a slight thing in the sight of the Lord* (2 Kings 3:18).

The miracle of supernatural provision.

A certain widow comes to Elisha for help. Her husband has died and left her owing debts she cannot pay. The creditors are threatening to take her two children as slaves. Elisha asks, "What do you have in the house?" In other words, what has God already given you? The widow has nothing, except one jar of oil. Elisha tells her to borrow as many empty jars as she can and fill the empty jars from what God has already provided. By faith, she obeys. The oil doesn't run out until every jar is full – more than enough to pay off her debts and provide for her family. Elisha didn't set up a "go-fund-me" account or take up an offering. He knew the power of the Holy Spirit that was upon him was willing and able to take what the widow poured out and multiply it abundantly. (2 Kings 4:1-7)

The miracle of supernatural life.

A Shunammite lady was blessed with a child after showing Elisha hospitality. When the child was old enough, he went out to the fields with his father, but suffered a terrible headache and died within hours. The woman didn't panic. She didn't call in the mourners. She laid the boy on Elisha's bed and rode quickly to find the prophet. When Elisha arrived, he stretched himself over the child, eye to eye, hand on hand, even mouth to mouth. It is as if he was sharing the power of God that resided in him through the Holy Spirit, and indeed, the child's body grew warm and he opened his eyes, brought back to life.

Faith Enacted

Faith in God is faith in the Holy Spirit. Elisha recognized from the first moment Elijah cast his cloak over him that, in himself, he possessed no power to do miracles and no words that would speak life to his people. He requested a double portion of the Holy Spirit's power, and indeed, received it by faith.

Give me a faith like Elisha. May we walk in the Spirit as He enlightens our minds and hearts to understand the Word of God, convicts us of sin, and directs our steps. We are not all called to be prophets, but as followers of Jesus, may we all desire a double portion of the powerful Spirit of God.

Luke 11:13 – *If you then, being evil, know how to give good gifts to your children, how much more will your heavenly Father give the Holy Spirit to those who ask Him?"*

Faith Expressed

Dear Father, How grateful we are that You sent the Holy Spirit to indwell Your people. We surrender ourselves to be used by Your Spirit. Like Elisha, we desire a double portion of Your power, so that we may serve you faithfully. In Jesus' Name, Amen.

DAY 34: GIVE ME A FAITH LIKE MICAH

But as for me, I will watch expectantly for the Lord;
I will wait for the God of my salvation.
My God will hear me.
–Micah 7:7

Faith Examined

If all we had to evaluate your faith by were the words you spoke, what kind of faith would be revealed? We know very little about the prophet Micah, only that he came from a town called Moresheth and his ministry took place in the days of King Jotham, Ahaz, and Hezekiah. God gave him a vision of what was to come on Samaria (the northern kingdoms of Israel) and Jerusalem (the southern kingdom of Judah). What we can know about his faith must be gleaned from the words he spoke.

While Micah describes the bad things that are going to happen as Israel is conquered and carried off into captivity, he also gives us a faith-filled picture of the God he served. Micah did not believe God is a distant, disconnected deity, only showing us our failures and sin and leaving us to fix ourselves. Instead, he recognized by faith that God is intimately involved in our restoration.

Here are six core beliefs of Micah's faith that we can see in the sermons he preached to his people.

Micah had faith to mourn the sin of his people.
When God opened Micah's eyes to the sinful rebellion of the people he lived among, Micah had two possible responses. He could have seen himself as righteous and taken on an attitude of condemnation toward others. Instead, he chose to mourn over their sin and what it was doing to their lives. He lamented. He wailed. He went barefoot and naked as a picture of repentance and sorrow for the wound that sin had created between God and His people. (Micah 1:8-9)

Micah had faith to see God's plan and purpose.
God gave Micah a glimpse of the coming millennial kingdom, when all will be restored under the rule of King Jesus. After describing the glory to come, he puts the coming judgment into perspective. The people will go to Babylon, but there they will be rescued. The nations who rejoice over Israel's calamity *do not know the thoughts of the Lord, and they do not understand His purpose.* God will thresh His people but, in the end, He will rescue, redeem and restore. (Micah 4)

Micah had faith to see Jesus.
Micah 5:2 is a key Messianic prophesy, one of hundreds of Old Testament prophesies that were fulfilled by Jesus and confirmed that He truly is the Son of God sent to accomplish salvation according to the predetermined plan of God. God reveals to Micah that Jesus will be born in Bethlehem.

Micah had faith to see God's grace.
Micah 6:8 is well-known and often chosen as one's "life verse." *He has told you, O man, what is good; and what does the Lord require of you but to do justice, to love kindness, and to walk humbly with your God?* Micah knew men were unable to keep God's law perfectly. In the same way that Jesus summed up the law in two simple commandments (love God first, love others as yourself), Micah realized the grace that was to come in the Messiah would enable men to please God by simply walking humbly and obediently.

Micah had faith to wait on God.
Micah knew that salvation would come, but it would come on God's timetable. He knew his people had sinned; he knew God was just and right to discipline them for it. He also understood that God would see them in the dark times and bring them back into the light. *Do not rejoice over me, O my enemy. Though I fall I will rise; though I dwell in darkness, the Lord is a light for me.* (Micah 7:8)

Micah had faith in the character of God.
The vision of judgment did not dismay Micah or cause his faith to falter. His faith rested not in the circumstances, but in the character of God. God was in covenant with His people, a covenant that was created because *God delights in unchanging love.* Micah could see past what would happen today or tomorrow because he had confidence in an eternal, unchanging God. (Micah 7:18-20)

Faith Enacted

Do you see the gospel in Micah's faith?
We must mourn over our personal and corporate sin.
We must acknowledge our Creator and His plans and purposes.
We must believe in Jesus, the Son of God, Messiah and Savior.
We must receive salvation as a gift of grace by faith.
We must wait on God to fulfill His eternal promises.
We must rest in the unchanging character of God.

Micah shows us that God brings the charge against us for our sin, and then steps in and pleads our case. This is what Jesus ultimately did on the cross. God's wrath poured out on His own Son reveals the dire circumstances of our sinful condition. Jesus pleads our case to His Father, taking our punishment so that we could be redeemed and restored, just as He promised. Give me a faith like Micah. Let me see God's grace in the discipline and have faith in His unchanging love that pursues us.

Micah 7:18 – *Who is a God like You, who pardons iniquity and passes over the rebellious act of the remnant of His possession? He does not retain His anger forever; because He delights in unchanging love.*

Faith Expressed

Dear Father, I'm so thankful for Your unchanging love that has pursued us since the beginning of Creation. Give us faith like Micah to mourn our sin, but also to accept the offer of grace and mercy through redemption in Christ. In Jesus' Name, Amen.

DAY 35: GIVE ME A FAITH LIKE NAHUM

The Lord is good, a stronghold in the day of trouble,
and He knows those who take refuge in Him.
But with an overflowing flood He will make a complete end of its site,
and will pursue His enemies into darkness.
–Nahum 1:7-8

Faith Examined

True faith in God is a faith that sees and acknowledges God in *all* His character. There's a tendency today to define faith as allegiance to Christianity but not to Christ. Christ is God's final word, the completion of the revelation of Himself to mankind. Jesus is the *radiance of His [God's] glory and the exact representation of His nature* (Hebrews 1:3), therefore, genuine, saving faith must accept God as revealed, not as we imagine Him to be.

This can be difficult, especially the view of God we see in the Old Testament as revealed by the prophets preaching God's coming judgment and discipline against sin and rebellion. But if we want real faith in the real God, we must study **all** scripture by asking, "What does this reveal about the character of God?"

Nahum doesn't disappoint us.

The prophet Nahum was sent to Nineveh, the capital city of the Assyrian empire. This took place about 150 years after the prophet Jonah was sent by God to preach to this wicked and cruel people, the enemy of His chosen people. On that occasion, both the people and the king believed Jonah's message and repented; God relented and withheld judgment. Now, a generation or more later, they have forgotten God. Nahum is commissioned to carry the news that judgment is coming.

Nahum's faith is not in the world's view of God as a weak and benevolent being whose only attribute is love and indulgence. Nahum reveals the real God.

Nahum's faith is in the God who is jealous and avenging; the God who takes vengeance on His foes and reserves His wrath for His enemies (1:2).

Nahum's faith is in the God who is slow to anger, yet who is great in power and will not leave the guilty unpunished (1:3).

Nahum's faith is in the God who is indignant against evil, yet He is good (1:6-7).

Nahum's faith is in the God who pursues His enemies into darkness, yet is a refuge for those who come to Him (1:7-8).

Twice in this little book of just three chapters, Nahum reveals something about God's character that should cause us to stop and take notice. He makes a sobering statement to Nineveh: "I am against you" (2:13,3:5). This is important when you consider that just over a hundred years earlier, Nineveh responded when Jonah brought a similar message, and God spared the city. When the king of Nineveh humbled his heart and led his people to repentance, God was "for" them. He forgave them, and withheld judgment. But, as a new generation took their place, they threw off the "burden" of God's commands and found themselves in opposition to the Most High God who had the power to destroy them for their sin.

Faith Enacted

It's easy to look at Jesus in the New Testament, full of grace and truth, and forget that *God is angry with the wicked every day* (Psalm 7:11 NKJV). Nahum reminds us that real faith requires accepting the God whose righteous and holy character is indignant about our sin, but also loves us deeply and is a refuge to those who repent.

All who profess faith in Jesus must come to terms that we are just like Nineveh, deserving of God's judgment. We were once enemies of God, but in Christ, we have been brought near and reconciled (Ephesians 2). How did this happen? The "enmity" between us and God was destroyed; the walls came down when Christ took our sin and bore the judgment of God for it on the cross. When we are made righteous in Christ, God is not angry nor indignant against us anymore; His wrath has been satisfied at the cross. God is our stronghold, for we have come to Him on His terms, through Jesus.

God's character never changes. When we willfully choose to remain in our sin, *He is against us.* In mercy and grace, He has provided a way to be brought back into the sanctuary of favor with Him, where *He is for us.*

Give me a faith like Nahum. Let my eyes be opened to the fullness of God's character, trusting in the completeness of His righteous judgment of sin at the cross of Jesus for all who put their faith in Him.

Romans 5:10 – *For if while we were enemies we were reconciled to God through the death of His Son, much more, having been reconciled, we shall be saved by His life.*

Faith Expressed

Dear Father, How grateful we are that Jesus took upon Himself Your wrath against the sins of the world. How humbled we are by Your love and Your willingness to forgive us of the things that offend Your righteous and holy nature. You are our refuge, but only through faith in Jesus. We never want to hear You say, "I am against You." Give us faith like Nahum to worship You fully for who You really are. In Jesus' Name, Amen.

DAY 36: GIVE ME A FAITH LIKE HABAKKUK

> Are you not from everlasting,
> O Lord, my God, my Holy One?
> We will not die.
> –Habakkuk 1:12a

Faith Examined

Habakkuk was a contemporary prophet of Jeremiah's, and he asks the questions that we all want to ask of God. "Why do You let wickedness and unrighteousness continue? Why do You choose to use the wicked to oppress and discipline Your people? How can You look at the evil that is going on in our world, and not do something about it?" (1:12-13)

Habakkuk sees a vision that God intends to bring the Chaldeans against Judah to punish and discipline His children. What he can't understand is that the Chaldeans are even more wicked than Israel. It seems odd that God would permit them to destroy, oppress, and persecute His own. Thankfully, God answers. One Bible scholar summed it up this way: *Evil, wherever it is found, always bears within it the seeds of its own destruction.* It doesn't matter where Israel's punishment comes from; it is inevitable, but *if the oppressors themselves are evil—as the Babylonians are—then they too will face their own destruction. Only in righteousness is there life; sin always brings death.*

The discipline of God can have two effects on us. Without faith, we respond in righteous indignation, questioning God's purposes as He deals with our sin. This response causes us to fall away. Habakkuk teaches us a better way as he shows us some key beliefs that will not only sustain our faith in God, but deepen and refine our faith under the Father's loving hand of chastisement and correction.

We must believe and live with an eternal perspective.
Habakkuk sees the destruction coming, and it's frightening. The enemy is fierce, and they are coming with violence to devour the land. If Habakkuk looked at the physical circumstances right in front of him, he would lose heart, but he has an eternal perspective. God is eternal; He is everlasting, and His people are hidden in Him. He says it simply, as a matter of fact: *We will not die* (1:12). Of course, many will die physically, but Habakkuk sees from an eternal perspective. *We will not die.*

We must trust in God's justice and leave the timing to Him.
Whatever evil is perpetrated on God's people will be turned back onto the oppressors. *The cup in the Lord's right hand will come around to you, and utter disgrace will come upon your glory* (2:16b). Where they disgrace others, they will be disgraced. Where they shed blood, their blood will be shed. Where they have done violence, violence will be done to them. Where they have plundered, they will be plundered. Habakkuk is told to wait because God's justice and righteousness will one

day prevail. *For the vision is yet for the appointed time; it hastens toward the goal and it will not fail* (2:3).

We must believe in God's glorious reign over earth.
When wickedness seems to be winning it's easy to lose faith. Habakkuk encourages us to look beyond what we can *see* and trust in what we *know. For the earth WILL be filled with the knowledge of the glory of the Lord, as the waters cover the sea* (2:14) There is a future reign of Christ yet to come – a visible, present kingdom with Jesus ruling from Jerusalem. That is enough for hope, but there's more. *But the Lord IS in His holy temple. Let all the earth be silent before Him* (2:20). God is ruling right now. Men may have the illusion they are in control, as the Chaldeans thought they were responsible for the conquest of Judah, but man is under God's authority, sovereignty and rule today; they just choose not to acknowledge it.

At the end of his prophecy, Habakkuk writes a beautiful prayer to the Lord that reads like a psalm – full of emotion and passion. He reminds us of all that God has done in the past for Israel and the mighty display of His power that gives us hope.

Faith Enacted

As we look around at the world today, we see that evil and wickedness grows more and more prevalent. God's people are persecuted, oppressed and many are dying for their faith even now. It often looks like evil is winning. Like Habakkuk, we "must wait quietly for the day of distress," confident in the same power that saved us to overcome the darkness around us.

Are you discouraged? Do you feel hopeless? Does it seem things will never change, but only get worse? Take heart. Remind yourself of all that God did to bring you to salvation and how He has changed your life. Trust in His timing to redeem all things.

Give me faith like Habakkuk. May we keep our eyes on eternity, trusting God's perfect timing to render justice to all the ungodly who stand in defiance against Him. Let us live in the knowledge that He rules and reigns with perfect wisdom.

Habakkuk 3:17-19 – *Though the fig tree should not blossom and there be no fruit on the vines, though the yield of the olive should fail and the fields produce no food, though the flock should be cut off from the fold and there be no cattle in the stalls, yet I will exult in the LORD, I will rejoice in the God of my salvation. The Lord God is my strength, and He has made my feet like hinds feet, and makes me walk on my high places.*

Faith Expressed

Dear Father, We trust in Your perfect justice. Whether we are on the receiving end of Your hand of discipline, or simply experiencing the effects of our enemy's influence in an ungodly and fallen world, we want to keep our eyes on You. Give us faith like Habakkuk. We have heard the report about You! Oh Lord, in wrath remember mercy. In Jesus' Name, Amen.

DAY 37: GIVE ME FAITH LIKE ASAPH

Whom have I in heaven but You?
And besides You, I desire nothing on earth.
My flesh and my heart may fail,
but God is the strength of my heart and my portion forever.
–Psalm 73:25-26

Faith Examined

Asaph was a Levite appointed by David as one of his chief worship leaders when the ark of the covenant was brought back into Jerusalem and set up in the Tent of Meeting (1 Chronicles 16:4-5). Asaph's sons and grandsons would have served in this same role in the Temple built by Solomon. We see his legacy continue even into the days of Ezra and Nehemiah, as his descendants reestablished and led the worship in the rebuilt Temple (Ezra 3:10). Asaph was the writer of some of the most beloved Psalms.

In 1 Chronicles 25:1-3, we learn that Asaph's role as a worship leader was more than just writing songs that stirred up the people emotionally. They were *set apart for the service...to **prophesy** with lyres, harps and cymbals.* They **prophesied** *in giving thanks and praising the Lord.* The words they wrote were just as inspired by the Holy Spirit of God as the word of Isaiah, or Daniel. *For no prophecy was ever made by an act of human will, but men moved by the Holy Spirit spoke from God.* (2 Peter 1:21).

The Hebrew word translated as prophesy is *nāḇā.* Strong's defines it as "to speak or sing by inspiration." It means "to pour forth words abundantly as is done by those who speak with ardor or divine emotion of mind, as a prophet is one who reveals or declares the words of God to man. It is to sing holy songs as led by the Spirit of God" (Gesenius' Hebrew-Chaldee Lexicon). Asaph spoke the words of God, only his were set to music.

There are twelve Psalms attributed to Asaph (Psalms 50 and 73-83). In them, we get a glimpse of the kind of faith that praises and glorifies God. Here are just four attributes of God, in whom Asaph's faith was securely anchored.

Asaph had faith in the self-sufficiency of God.
If I were hungry I would not tell you, for the world is Mine, and all it contains. God needs nothing from us, but He desires our sacrifices of thanksgiving and praise (Psalm 50:10-14). Asaph had faith that God was completely satisfied in Himself, and completely self-existent. God is and has all that He will ever need, and we are dependent on Him for our existence. Our faith is not in a God who is just a "better version" of ourselves; God is transcendent. *You thought that I was just like you; I will reprove you and state the case in order before your eyes* (Psalm 50:21).

Asaph had faith in the supremacy of God.
Eight times in twelve psalms, Asaph refers to God as the Most High. He includes this title in his first psalm: *Pay your vows to the Most High* (50:14), and the very last verse of his very last psalm recorded in scripture ends this way: *That they may know that You alone, whose name is the Lord, are the Most High over all the earth* (83:18). Asaph had a right perspective of God. There is no other God. There is no one higher, no one more powerful, no greater authority than the God of Abraham, Isaac, and Jacob – the God who created you and me and rules supreme over all of time and space, and all that exists. Our faith rests in the *Most High God.*

Asaph had faith in the sovereignty of God.
Psalm 73 tells the story of Asaph's struggle to understand God's purposes. When his eyes are on the things of this world and the people around him, he *comes close to stumbling* in his faith. The ungodly are prosperous, yet the godly suffer. It troubles him until he comes into the sanctuary of God. Here, as he worships, God gives him a glimpse of his future and he perceives the end of the wicked. He made the Lord God his refuge, and when all of God's sovereign plans are fulfilled, God will receive him to glory, but the wicked will perish.

Asaph had faith in the steadfastness of God.
If there was one thought that undergirded all that Asaph wrote, it would be a sure confidence in the covenant-keeping nature of God, even in times of suffering. *Has God forgotten to be gracious, or has He in anger withdrawn His compassion? Then I said, "It is my grief, that the right hand of the Most High has changed"* (Psalm 77:9-10). Whenever Asaph's faith faltered, he returned repeatedly to worship the unchangeable nature of God. The emotions of grief, fear, and uncertainty can be overcome by faith in the steadfastness of our God.

Faith Enacted

Asaph shows us that whether our words are set to music, or written as poetry, or simply spoken, true, prophetic, God-inspired worship must be rooted in a right concept of God. He is self-existent and self-sufficient. He is supreme over all gods. He is sovereign and His plans for mankind will be fulfilled just as He has ordained. He is steadfast and we can build our faith on the knowledge that God keeps His covenant.

Give me a faith like Asaph. May we sing and speak of God as He is. This is where true faith rests.

Psalm 79:9-10a – *Help us, O God of our salvation, for the glory of Your name; and deliver us and forgive our sins for Your name's sake. Why should the nations say, "Where is their God?"*

Faith Expressed

Dear Father, Oh, how we look forward to gathering around Your throne and worshipping You in all of Your holiness and glory! Until then, teach us how to express our faith in ways that honor and praise You for who You truly are. In Jesus' Name, Amen.

DAY 38: GIVE ME A FAITH LIKE HAGGAI

And the elders of the Jews were successful in building through the
prophesying of Haggai the prophet and Zechariah the son of Iddo. And they
finished building according to the command of the God of Israel and the
decree of Cyrus, Darius, and Artaxerxes of Persia.
–Ezra 6:14

Faith Examined

The prophets Haggai and Zechariah were contemporaries who returned to Jerusalem with the exiles. While we don't know for sure, Haggai was probably in his eighties. He likely saw the destruction of Jerusalem; he remembered the former glory of the beautiful city and Temple.

God used Haggai to stir up His people at a critical time. They were discouraged, having been prevented from continuing the work of the rebuilding the Temple. As time passed, the people abandoned the project and forgot the reason God sent them back to the homeland. They were busy building their own homes and planting crops. The house of the Lord lay desolate, and seemingly, no one was concerned.

Haggai brings a strong message from the Lord to awaken the people from their apathy. He exposes the reason they are struggling in their personal lives; they have neglected what matters to God. God had caused a drought to get their attention, but they weren't listening. The harder they worked, the less they accomplished. They planted much, but harvested little. They ate, but never had enough. They put on clothes, but were not warm. God says, *You expected much, but see, it turned out to be little. What you brought home, I blew away.* He tells them why: *Because of my house, which remains a ruin, while each of you is busy with your own house* (Haggai 1:9 NIV).

Haggai was personally invested in the Temple project. Haggai 2:3 seems to imply that he had seen the former Temple before it was destroyed, and he recognized that the one they were building paled in comparison. He knew some of the people were discouraged. He didn't simply preach to the people about their sins and walk away; he stayed with them and supported them until the task was done (Ezra 5:1-2).

Haggai not only addressed the common people, but took his message to Zerubbabel, the governor, and Joshua, the high priest. He knew if they listened and obeyed God's words of warning and rebuke, the people would follow. It took courage to address those in places of authority, as it was their decisions that allowed the work to stop.

Thankfully, both the governor and the high priest responded, and led the people to repent in reverence to the Lord. They renewed their commitment and work began again. God provided for *all* their needs as they moved forward to do His work, and the Temple was rebuilt for God's glory.

Faith Enacted

What do we learn about faith from Haggai?

First, as we see in all of God's prophets, we must be willing to challenge our fellow believers according to God's Word, but we must speak humbly and with love. As followers of Jesus, we don't always get things right. We need pastors and teachers who aren't afraid to point out the areas in our lives where we may be missing the mark. We must also be men and women of faith who are willing to support, stand by, and do the hard work with others, just as Haggai did for his people. We can have the boldest faith in the room, but if we're not humble enough to serve, we won't have much influence on the hearts of God's people.

Secondly, we need to examine our own faith for any areas where we've put our personal priorities in front of God's kingdom work. When we find ourselves struggling to "make life work," will we realize we have neglected the things that matter to God and that in love and grace He's trying to get our attention? If we let our spiritual lives "lie desolate" and focus all our energy and attention on our physical lives of work, school, family, home, and career, then church and worship may become optional, and ultimately abandoned. We will be negligent in prayer. God's Word will become irrelevant. If these things happen, we shouldn't be surprised when life gets more and more difficult.

Jesus put it this way: *Do not worry then, saying, 'What will we eat' or 'What will we drink?' or 'What will we wear for clothing?' For the Gentiles eagerly seek all these things; for your heavenly Father knows that you need all these things. But seek first His kingdom and His righteousness, and all these things will be added to you* (Matthew 6:31-33).

We're not building a physical temple; we are the temple of God. We're building lives that are meant to reflect the glory of God and point others to Him. Are we concerned about His Kingdom, or ours? An honest examination will reveal if what matters to Him, matters to us. Give me a faith like Haggai, and may I never abandon what's important to God.

Haggai 1:4-5 – *Is it time for you yourselves to dwell in your paneled houses while this house lies desolate? Now therefore, thus says the Lord of hosts, "Consider your ways!"*

Faith Expressed

Dear Father, How easy it is to be distracted by the responsibilities and pleasures of this physical life, and forget our first priority is Your house, Your kingdom, and the good works You planned for us to walk in for Your glory. Forgive us when we neglect what matters to You. May we be faithful and bold like Haggai to tell our brothers and sisters the truth. May we be willing to serve alongside those who are struggling in support and encouragement and be humble enough to recognize our own failures when others confront us. May we be faithful to You and You alone. In Jesus' Name, Amen.

DAY 39: GIVE ME FAITH LIKE ZECHARIAH

Therefore say to them, "Thus says the Lord of hosts,
'Return to Me,' declares the Lord of hosts,
'that I may return to you,' says the Lord of hosts."
–Zechariah 1:3

Faith Examined

As a descendant of Levi and part of the priestly tribe, Zechariah lived in an exciting time. Born into Babylonian captivity, he participated in the first return of the Jewish exiles to their homeland, after God stirred up the spirit of King Cyrus to release them.

Not everyone wanted to return to Jerusalem. Many had died during captivity, and the older generation was certainly aware of the devastation that awaited them. They had seen the destruction of their beloved Temple; they had witnessed the raping and pillaging of their people. Surely these memories made many hesitate to sign up for the return. But I imagine the younger generation was full of hope and ready for the adventure. As one who inherited priestly responsibilities, Zechariah was part of an elite group. When the rebuilt Temple became a reality and sacrifices were restored, the duties performed by the Zechariah would be essential in the worship of Yahweh.

Upon their arrival in Jerusalem, the first thing to be rebuilt was the altar, so the sacrifices prescribed by God could resume. For seventy years, the people had not had a way to atone for their sins. Jeshua (Joshua) the priest and Zerubbabel the governor knew this was important, even before the foundations of the Temple were laid. The people needed to be restored to fellowship with God. By the second year, the foundations were complete, and the people celebrated.

As always, the joy of God's people aroused the enemy's attention. The mixed race of Samaritans, remnants of the Assyrian captivity, wanted to join the work, but Joshua and Zerubbabel wisely declined the offer. Offended, the people of the land began to discourage and frighten the Jews; finally, they resorted to political maneuvers, and the construction stopped.

It is in this climate that God begins to use Zechariah as His prophet. The people are discouraged. Fear has once again brought disobedience as they abandon the work, and their lives are no longer centered on worshipping God.

It took twenty-four years from the arrival of the first returning exiles in Jerusalem to the completion of the Temple (539-515 BC). When the people abandoned God, He did not abandon them, but sent His prophet Zechariah to stir up their hearts. Again and again, he cried out, urging the people to return to the Lord and finish the work even though they faced insurmountable physical circumstances and cultural pressures from the surrounding enemies.

Zechariah 1:16-17 – *Therefore thus says the Lord, "I will return to Jerusalem with compassion; My house will be built in it," declares the Lord of hosts, "and a measuring line will be stretched over Jerusalem." Again, proclaim, saying, "Thus says the Lord of hosts, "My cities will again overflow with prosperity, and the Lord will again comfort Zion and again choose Jerusalem."*

Zechariah sees that God will use Joshua to finish the work, as an angel of the Lord admonishes Joshua in a vision: *Thus says the Lord of hosts, "If you will walk in My ways and if you will perform My service, then you will also govern My house and also have charge of My courts, and I will grant you free access among these who are standing here"* (Zechariah 3:7).

Zechariah also proclaims God's prophecies over Zerubbabel, His chosen servant for this time: *Then he said to me, "This is the word of the Lord to Zerubbabel saying, 'Not by might not by power, but by My Spirit,' says the Lord of hosts. ... The hands of Zerubbabel have laid the foundation of this house, and his hands will finish it. Then you will know that the Lord of hosts has sent me to you."* (Zechariah 4:6,9).

Faith Enacted

What great faith Zechariah had in God's revealed will and plans for His people! His faithfulness to keep speaking, keep encouraging, keep pushing his people to finish the work was greatly used by God. In his later years, Zechariah would prophesy things not yet fulfilled, and it is these prophecies that encourage *our* generation to work faithfully and obediently until Jesus returns.

Here are two takeaways from Zechariah's life of faith. First, when we are discouraged, we can go to the words of the prophets and be reminded that *God always keeps His word.* No matter what the world says or how bleak or frightening the circumstances may be, God always fulfills what He has promised to His people.

Second, we need to be faithful encouragers to our brothers and sisters. There is Kingdom work to be done, and as we draw closer to our Lord's return, it's all hands on deck to finish the mission. May we have faith like Zechariah to hold one another accountable and keep our eyes on the finish line.

Zechariah 8:9 – *Thus says the Lord of hosts, "Let your hands be strong, you who are listening in these days to these words from the mouth of the prophets, those who spoke in the day that the foundation of the house of the Lord of hosts was laid, to the end that the temple might be built."*

Faith Expressed

Dear Father, How grateful we are for the assurance that You always keep Your promises. We can look forward to the restoration of all things with confidence because You are faithful to restore what was lost in past generations. We look forward to the final restoration Zechariah speaks of. May we confidently serve you in faith until all is fulfilled. In Jesus' Name, Amen.

Day 40: Give Me A Faith Like Malachi

Then those who feared the Lord spoke to one another,
and the Lord gave attention and heard it,
and a book of remembrance was written before Him
for those who fear the Lord and who esteem His name.
–Malachi 3:16

Faith Examined

We don't know very much about the man, Malachi. He received his word from God around 440-400 BC, and has the distinction of being the very last of God's prophets to speak before the four hundred years of silence that preceded Christ's first coming. Malachi's *message*, however, has much to teach us about faith.

God called Malachi to address three main issues with His people, and it's worth noting they were not easy ones to confront. The people were disrespecting God in their worship; they were dealing treacherously with one another in relationships; and they were robbing God with their money. Malachi teaches us that the kind of faith that pleases God is practical in all matters. Real faith that fears God and esteems His name isn't something we practice half-heartedly. It begins with our worship, carries over into our relationships, and governs our stewardship of God's blessings.

Faithless Worship

The real culprits in Israel's failure to worship God properly were their religious leaders, the priests. They were failing to teach truth and were allowing corrupt sacrifices. The people had grown selfish and lazy and were bringing the worst of their flocks and fields to God's altar, revealing not only did they not respect God, but they also despised Him. *My, how tiresome it is!* they said to God. They profaned the table of the Lord.

God required the sacrifices to be blameless, holy, and without spot or blemish, because each one was a picture of the sacrifice His Son would make on the cross for the sins of the world. The people had forgotten their sins separated them from God; they treated worship as an afterthought, and the sacrifices as mundane and optional.

Faithless Relationships

God had repeatedly warned His people not to marry into other cultures who worshipped foreign gods, but they had ignored His instructions. Not only that, but they were also divorcing their wives, making a mockery of marriage. They wearied God with their words, calling those who did evil as good, and claiming God delighted in their evil. When God did not accept their offerings, they wept and groaned, failing to recognize their own sin, and instead blaming God. They broke God's covenant, but were confused when He withheld blessing from their lives.

Faithless Stewardship

The people Malachi confronted had failed to give back to God what belonged to Him – the tithes and offerings. They were arrogant, saying it was vain to serve God, and brought them no profit. Their actions were bringing a curse on the nation. They were literally robbing God.

Faith Enacted

Malachi's words are challenging for us today. We, too, are often tempted to push worship to the side, take it for granted, or participate half-heartedly. We seek our own good in relationships, and by and large, think little of divorcing our spouse to fulfill our own desires. We take God's blessings as something we've earned or deserved, and instead of seeing all of our possessions as belonging to Him, we make our pleasure and comfort a priority over kingdom stewardship.

Thankfully, Malachi's message also tells us how to restore our faith. First, God reminded the people, *I have loved you* (1:2). As followers of Jesus, we are saved, born again into a covenant relationship with God. He loves us, just as He loved the children of Israel. Knowing we are loved by God helps us do what is required when we admit our faithless actions – *Return to Me, and I will return to you* (3:7).

The people who received Malachi's message changed their attitudes and behavior. They feared the Lord, and esteemed His name, and God took note of their repentance. *The Lord gave attention and heard it.* He wrote it down in His book of remembrance, which I believe is the book from which believers will give account of our lives (Romans 14:12). The result was a renewed faith – a faith that feared the Lord and esteemed His name – a faith that pleased God.

How's your worship? Do you bring faithful obedience and humility to God?

How are your relationships? Do they reflect the faith of a follower of Jesus?

How's your attitude toward money? Do you see all that you own as belonging to God, and your role as simply the faithful steward of His Kingdom resources?

Give me a faith like Malachi – faith that fears the Lord and esteems His name – the name that is great among the nations.

Malachi 1:11 – *For from the rising of the sun even to its setting, My name will be great among the nations ... says the Lord of hosts.*

Faith Expressed

Dear Father, We want a faith that proclaims Your name, not only in our words, but in the actions we take and the attitudes of our hearts. May our worship be pleasing and show respect to You. May we honor You in our relationships and be faithful and generous as we manage the blessings You have given us for Your kingdom purposes. Give us faith that pleases You and esteems Your name above all. In Jesus' Name, Amen.

A FINAL WORD: NOW WHAT?

If you are a follower of Jesus, my hope is that you have been blessed and renewed in your understanding of the faith that comes through a relationship with Him. If you are not a believer in Jesus, the first step to experiencing the faith described in this devotional is to respond to His offer of salvation by grace through faith. The Bible is clear that the only way to heaven is through Jesus. Here is how you can begin a relationship with Him.

Acknowledge that God created you for a relationship with Him.
Genesis 1:27 – *God created man in His own image, in the image of God He created him; male and female He created them.*
Colossians 1:16c – *All things have been created through Him and for Him.*

Admit that you are separated from God.
Romans 3:10-12,23 – *There is none righteous, not even one. There is none who understands, there is none who seeks for God...there is none who does good, there is not even one. ... For all have sinned and fall short of the glory of God.*

Believe Jesus is God's Son, that He died on the cross and rose from the grave.
Romans 10:9-10 – *That if you confess with your mouth Jesus as Lord, and believe in your heart that God raised Him from the dead, you will be saved; for with the heart a person believes, resulting in righteousness, and with the mouth he confesses, resulting in salvation.*

Confess your sin to God and turn away it.
1 John 1:9 – *If we confess our sins, He is faithful and righteous to forgive us our sins and to cleanse us from all unrighteousness.*

Receive Jesus as Lord of your life through the Holy Spirit.
John 1:12 – *But as many as received Him, to them He gave the right to become children of God, even to those who believe in His name.*
John 3:16 – *For God so loved the world, that He gave His only begotten Son, that whoever believes in Him shall not perish but have eternal life.*

What To Pray
Dear Jesus, I recognize that I am separated from You because of my personal sin, and I need Your forgiveness. I believe that You died on the cross to pay the penalty for my sin. I confess my sin and ask You to forgive me. By faith, I turn from my way of life to follow You and accept Your gift of salvation by grace. I ask You to come into my life and transform me. Thank You for saving me and giving me eternal life. In Jesus' Name, Amen.

If you sincerely prayed this prayer and surrendered your life to God, you are now His child. Please share this decision with another believer and ask him or her to help you get started in how to walk in your new life in Christ. We would love to hear about your decision!

ADDITIONAL RESOURCES

Going Around The Corner Bible Study
ISBN: 9780692781999 / List Price: $12.99
This six-session workbook helps believers explore the mission field in their own neighborhoods and workplaces. Learn to engage others through prayer and biblical good works guided by the prompts of the Holy Spirit. Gain confidence to evangelize through sharing the complete gospel and your own story. Discover how to establish and equip new believers in their faith journey. A simple, practical, and biblical strategy for disciple-making.

Going Around The Corner Bible Study, Student Edition
ISBN: 9780692781999 / List Price: $10.99
A five-session workbook developed for high school and college students. Covers the first four chapters of the adult study with expanded commentary and application focused on reaching the campus, dorm, and playing field for Christ. Students will be guided into God's Word and develop an awareness and passion for sharing the gospel.

Going Around The Corner Bible Study, Leader Guide
ISBN: 9780999131824 / List Price: $3.99
Key truths, discussion starters and thoughtful questions to facilitate group study, plus suggested activities, and practical application steps.

Going Around The Corner: The Guidebook
ISBN: 9781733047821 / List Price: $6.99
This little guidebook helps you take what you know about the gospel and share it. Take one step at a time and implement it. Soon you will love the people God has put in your life with Christ's love and will be interceding on their behalf. You will get to know them personally and be involved in their lives. You will be confident in sharing your own conversion story and the complete gospel. You will be the one to introduce them to Jesus.

40 Days of Spiritual Awareness
ISBN: 9780999131800 / List Price: $9.99
Understand who God is and how He is working in the people right around you. Discover truth that will increase your awareness of God, yourself, other believers, and unbelievers. Be reminded of God's work in our world, as He redeems and saves. At the end of the 40-day journey, you will realize that you are an important part of accomplishing that work and be prepared to join Him.

Grace & Glory: A 50-Day Journey In The Purpose & Plan Of God
ISBN: 9780999131848 / List Price $11.99
What do we do when we face a crisis of faith? When everything we believe is challenged? That's when we must discover (or re-discover) God's purpose for our lives and learn to live with a mindset of His grace...grace that reveals His glory. This devotional will refresh believers in the gospel and encourage them to live every day so that the glory of God will be proclaimed by the power of grace at work in their lives.

Just Pray: God's Not Done With You
ISBN: 9780999131886 / List Price $9.99
How often have you heard someone say, "All I can do is 'just pray'!" The reality is, the most powerful and effective thing we can do is pray. You are strategically, sovereignly positioned to have kingdom impact in this generation through a simple commitment to prayer. God is not looking for people of strength and confidence. He is seeking those who know they are helpless and weak so that His strength and glory can be made magnified in them. No matter what your limitations, God still has work for you to do for the kingdom. We invite you to accept the challenge and just pray.

Let Us Run The Race
ISBN: 9781733047807 / List Price $9.99
The greatest missionary of all time, Paul made an unforgettable and enduring impact on the culture that surrounded him. If we could sit down and chat with him, what would he tell us? What can we learn from a man who ran his race so well? We all want our lives to count for something greater than ourselves. The reality is, there is no greater call than the cause of Christ and the gospel of His kingdom. Let's pursue Him with passion, endurance, and joy. Let's run the race, for Jesus is worthy.

Living In Light of the Manger
ISBN: 9780999131817 / List Price $9.99
If the manger only has meaning during our holiday celebrations, we've missed the point of the story. Jesus was born, so that we could be *born again.* The events of His birth and the people who welcomed Him have many lessons to teach us about the glorious gospel and how Jesus came to change our lives. Discover the purpose and power of the manger. Perfect as a gift to introduce the gospel to friends, co-workers, and neighbors.

Open The Gift
ISBN: 9781733047869 / List Price $9.99
Salvation isn't just something that makes us better, kinder people while we live here and guarantees us a blissful eternity when we die. It's a whole new life. It's a gift that we keep opening as we discover who Jesus really is and what He came to give us. Do you know what you have in Jesus?

One-To-One Discipleship
ISBN: MM121 / List Price $17.00
A nine-session course for one believer to establish a new believer in the Christian faith, covering nine foundational stones upon which to build the new life in Christ. The biblical foundations of Assurance, Attributes of God, the Bible, Prayer, Spirit-Filled Life, Witnessing, Temptation, and Obedience contribute to a solid beginning for a new believer. Published by Multiplication Ministries and available from ATCM. A women's edition is also available. Used worldwide, this resource has sold over a million copies since it was written.

All resources are available on our website: aroundthecornerministries.org

About The Author

Sheila Alewine was raised in a Christian home where she came to faith in Christ at an early age. She met her husband, Todd, while attending Liberty University in Lynchburg, VA. They married in 1985 and have spent their lives serving God together.

As a young mom, Sheila fell in love with Bible study when asked to join a Precept study. Throughout the years of raising their daughters, working full-time, and serving in ministry, she has loved studying and teaching in the Word. She writes for two reasons: to encourage those who know Jesus to serve Him passionately and tell others about Him; and to invite those who do not yet believe to consider Christ.

Sheila and her husband reside in Hendersonville, NC, where they have established *Around The Corner Ministries* to equip and encourage followers of Christ to share the gospel where they live, work and play. They love spending time with their daughters, sons-in-law, and grandchildren.

Contact Us

Sheila writes regularly on her blog, *The Way of the Word* (sheilaalewine.com) and for the Crossway group (biblestudytools.com). You can connect with her through their ministry website (aroundthecornerministries.org) or find her on Facebook and Instagram.

If this devotional has made an impact on your life, please let us know by contacting us through our website **aroundthecornerministries.org**, by email to sheila@aroundthecornerministries.org, or through our Facebook page.

Around The Corner Ministries exists to take the gospel to every neighborhood in America. Our mission is to equip followers of Jesus to engage their neighborhoods and communities with the gospel of Jesus Christ.

Around The Corner Ministries is a partner to the local church, designed to teach and train Christ-followers how to evangelize their neighborhoods, workplaces, and communities. The goal is to grow healthy local churches filled with mature believers who are comfortable and passionate about sharing their faith. If you would like more information on how our ministry can partner with your local church, please contact us.